Cat Lover's Trivia

Cat Lover's Trivia

WEIRD AND WACKY FACTS
ABOUT OUR FURRY FRIENDS

MIKE DARTON

chartwell
books

© 2017 Quarto Publishing plc

This edition published in 2021 by Chartwell Books,
an imprint of The Quarto Group
142 West 36th Street, 4th Floor
New York, NY 10018 USA
T (212) 779-4972 F (212) 779-6058
www.QuartoKnows.com

Originally published by Ivy Press in 2009 as *Socks' Feline Miscellany*.

10 9 8 7 6 5 4 3 2 1

Chartwell titles are also available at discount for retail, wholesale, promotional, and bulk
purchase. For details, contact the Special Sales Manager by email at specialsales@quarto.
com or by mail at The Quarto Group, Attn: Special Sales Manager, 100 Cummings
Center Suite 265D, Beverly, MA 01915, USA.

ISBN: 978-0-7858-4017-6

Library of Congress Control Number: 2021936390

This book was conceived, designed and produced by
Ivy Press
Creative Director Peter Bridgewater
Publisher Jason Hook
Editorial Director Tom Kitch
Senior Editor Polita Caaveiro
Designer Richard Constable
Illustrations Ivan Hissey, Sarah Skeate & other old moggies

Printed in China

'A cat's got her own opinion of human beings.
She don't say much, but you can tell enough to make
you anxious not to hear the whole of it.'

JEROME K. JEROME

CURRENT MEMBERS of the cat family Felidae are divided into two subfamilies: the Pantherinae and the Felinae. Until recently, the cheetahs were believed to belong to a third, separate subfamily (known as the Acinonychinae) but DNA testing now suggests a close relationship with pumas. Also now known to be closely related to pumas is the so-called onza (wild cat) of Mexico. The grouping below combines the traditional taxonomic divisions of the Felidae arranged according to current DNA genetic evidence.

PANTHERINAE

genus *Panthera*	genus *Uncia*	genus *Neofelis*
lion	snow leopard	clouded leopard
leopard		Bornean clouded
jaguar		leopard
tiger		

FELINAE, OCELOT GROUP
genus *Leopardus*

Pantanal cat	kodkod	ocelot
colocolo	Andean mountain cat	oncilla
Geoffroy's cat	pampas cat	margay

FELINAE, PANTHERA GROUP

genus *Leptailurus*	genus *Caracal*	genus *Profelis*
serval	caracal	African golden cat

genus *Pardofelis*	genus *Catopuma*	
marbled cat	bay cat	
	Asian golden cat	

genus *Lynx*	genus *Puma*	genus *Prionailurus*
Canadian lynx	puma	leopard cat
Eurasian lynx	jaguarundi	Iriomote cat
Iberian lynx		flat-headed cat
bobcat	(genus *Acinonyx*)	rusty spotted cat
	cheetah	fishing cat

FELINAE PROPER
genus *Felis*

Chinese desert cat	black-footed cat	The genus *Felis* is now known to be genetically closely related to the three genera above, formerly classified as Pantherinae.
jungle cat	wild cat	
Pallas's cat	**domestic cat**	
sand cat		

Depending on where you are in the world, a black cat crossing your path in daylight hours can be incredibly lucky or unlucky. Of course it depends also on how superstitious you are (and on your memory for cats and, indeed, the paths you have trodden or feel you shouldn't have).

But in respect of their reputation as lucky or unlucky, cats have always been creatures of the night, and black cats are naturally that much less distinguishable at night. That is why by surprisingly recent tradition they have been associated with witches, who apparently ferried them around the skies at night-time on broomsticks (surely a highly insecure mode of transportation), when witches were themselves comparatively invisible. In fact, cats – black or any other colour – were not associated with witches in earlier centuries as much as other creatures nominated as 'familiars'.

SCENTS & SENSIBILITY

To be aware of their environment, cats rely on their sense of smell far more than their eyesight. That is why cats not only have between four and 14 times as many olfactory sensors (smell-receptor cells) in their noses as do humans, they make good use of the additional scent-analyzing organ in the roof of the mouth called the vomeronasal or Jacobson's organ. Other mammals and reptiles also have this organ – in humans, for example, it is used for the subliminal, even subconscious, detection of instinctual pheromones – but cats can particularly be seen to make use of theirs when encountering a strong and unfamiliar odour: they draw back the lips and wrinkle the nose in what is known as the 'flehmen response', which wafts the scent into the mouth and straight to the requisite analytical area.

SHOW BUSINESS

The first official cat show seems to have taken place at Crystal Palace, London, in 1871, although some authorities on the subject suggest that there was another cat show virtually simultaneously in Maine, New England, USA. Be that as it may, the rules for entering a cat in a show and the ways in which a show is organized differ from nation to nation and even sometimes from region to region. In the UK, the body responsible for the show rules is the Governing Council of the Cat Fancy (GCCF); in the USA it is the Cat Fanciers' Association that sets the breed standards and arranges the times and venues of shows. Generally, however, there are four main classes in which cats are shown: the kitten class (aged less than 10 months), the neutered class, the open class, and the household pet class (for neutered non-pedigree cats).

PUSS IN BOOTS

PUSS IN BOOTS is the English title of a nursery story translated into many languages but originally written in French (as *Le Chat Botté*) by Charles Perrault and published in his *Mother Goose Tales* in 1697. The French word for 'cat' became the English 'puss', often found in stories for late nineteenth-century nursery children. In the story, a wily cat manages to procure for his master, 'the Marquess of Carabas', the favour of the king and the hand of his daughter, the princess. It was first printed in English (translated by Andrew Lang) in 1889. It is significant to the story that the boots are not just any old boots but 'top-boots', the boots of a horse-rider and thus of a gentleman or of a gentleman's superior valet. *Puss in Boots* has been the subject of several animated films in the USA, Europe and Japan.

LET SLEEPING CATS LIE

Mature cats in good health sleep for about 65% of lives – 50% dozing or in light sleep, and 15% in deep sleep. That means they spend just 35% of their lives awake and alert, often calculated as an average seven hours a day. But despite this predilection for slumber, cats are said to wake from sleep to full alertness faster than any other animal. (Moreover, only 7% of cats snore, whereas 21% of dogs do.)

ERIE ORIGINS

Erie County, Ohio, USA, is named after the historic presence of the Erie Native American Indians. The name 'Erie' is almost always said to mean 'cat', and the county's name is said to derive from the Huron *eriche* or *erige*, or 'lake of the cats'. The cats involved in these references are held to be a particular species of wild cats that used to frequent the area. French maps drawn by early colonial explorers in the area certainly describe Lake Erie as *le Lac du Chat*, 'the Lake of the Cat'. But that is probably where the mistake began. For the Huron word that is now the name Erie in fact means 'raccoon'. It is a raccoon – not a cat – that features on the Erie Indians' totem poles. And raccoons are related to ringtails (and even bears and badgers) more closely than they are to cats. It is another example – like polecats and meerkats, neither of which are cats either – of how hopeless Europeans in previous centuries were at distinguishing between animals, lumping them together under one description.

As of 2007:

in the USA		in Australia	
MALE	**FEMALE**	**MALE**	**FEMALE**
Max	Princess	Oscar	Misty
Simba	Sophie/Sophia	Max	Coco
Sam	Molly	Sam	Chloe
Oliver	Cleo/Chloe	Simba	Lucy
Oscar	Maggie	Milo	Missy
Buddy	Lucy	Sooty	Molly

THE BIBLICAL LION

THE JUDAEO-CHRISTIAN BIBLE mentions the word 'lion' in the singular 82 times. This includes references not just to the tribe of Judah and its kings, described as terrible to their enemies and dealing with them as forcefully as a lion might, and to Jesus as an invincible lion of that same tribe, but also to the devil as a fierce and hungry lion seeeking to ensnare and destroy humans, and to enemies and evils of every kind – with similar propensities.

VAN PATTERN

The Van pattern is a coloration pattern for cats that comprises mainly white, but with the head and tail solid or tortoise-shell coloured. The pattern – which is alternatively known as the Seychellois pattern – is caused by the presence of the dominant gene for 'white spotting' in the cat's genetic make-up. It is called the Van pattern because it was first associated with the cats that lived in the area of Van, in eastern Turkey, close to the border with Iran. The place-name itself may well derive from Old Persian and have something to do with the close proximity of the large stretch of inland water known in English as Lake Van.

CATNIP

Nepeta cataria , or catnip, is known in the USA as catmint, which is in fact the original Middle English name for the European plant – a fairly direct translation from medieval botanical Latin *herba catti* or *herba cattaria*, thus also modern German *Katzenmünze*. Many (but not all) cats react strongly and apparently favourably to the catnip weed for several minutes at a time in what is thought to be an inherited hormonal response to the vapour of the terpene nepetalactone in the plant, although scent as such is not involved at all.

What is known in Europe as the *Cat Waltz*, by Frédéric Chopin (Opus 34, No.3, in French as *Valse brillante*) is said to have been partly composed after Chopin's cat jumped up onto his piano and ran along the keyboard. The apparently intrigued composer then tried to reproduce the string of notes the cat had sounded. It's a good story but does not explain how Monsieur Chopin also wrote *Dog Waltz* (better known as *The Minute Waltz*) and *Hamster Waltz*. While on the subject let us not ignore Scarlatti's *Cat Fugue*, the *Comic Duet for Two Cats* ascribed to Rossini, Martinu's *March of the Cats*, Ravel's *Cat Duet*, and John Cage's *Little Four Paws*.

BELL THE CAT

THIS STORY IS A FABLE, possibly originally by Aesop, but retold and popularized by William Langland in his *Vision of Piers Plowman* in the second half of the fourteenth century. The mouse family are desperate to find a way to warn themselves of the approach of the house cat, and come to the conclusion that the best method would be to hang a bell around its neck. All agree on this, until the wisest mouse asks who is actually going to put the bell on the cat – and, unsurprisingly, no one offers to perform the task.

The expression thus refers to both a heroic offer to do something suicidal, and to a situation in which there seems only a suicidal solution.

LAMENT FOR THE DEPARTED

'My husband said it was him or the cat. I miss him sometimes.'
ANONYMOUS

FELINE NORMALS

The normal body temperature of a household cat is 38–39.2° Celsius (100.5–102.5° Fahrenheit), and generally towards the higher end. The normal respiratory rate of a cat when resting is 16–40 breaths a minute. This is a wide range and observers should take into account any unusual or external factors that may appertain a different rate. The normal pulse rate of a cat at rest is 120–140 beats per minute, although a cat that is anticipating or receiving human attention may have a pulse rate considerably higher – it is said that the average pulse rate of a cat over a day may be as high as around 195–200 beats per minute.

ONE WAY OF CLASSIFYING CATS (for cat shows and for other purposes) is by the length of their fur. Indeed, because the cat's coat significantly affects a cat show judge's impression of the cat's overall size and shape, it may be regarded as one of a cat's most important features.

Long-haired cats may not only look very different underneath all that fur but may look different at different times of the year as hair is shed or regrows.

On short-haired cats you can see the shape of the body more clearly – but the texture of the coat may vary across the body in density, thickness and straightness.

Only one pedigree cat may be described as 'hairless' – and even then the Sphynx is not welcomed in shows all over the world. These cats do have short, downy fur at the extremities of the body.

The *texture* of the coat is a further consideration for judges when assessing any cat in a show.

A SPECIES OF ANY ANIMAL is generally defined as a group that breeds and produces fertile offspring. However, under artificial conditions – such as when kept in captivity – it is possible to cross-breed different species and create variants. For example, leopards have been crossed with lions to create leopons, lions with tigers to create ligers (father a lion) or tigons (father a tiger). The offspring are almost always sterile. The recent DNA clarification of the closeness of genetic groups has, meanwhile, proved why some hybridizations have been far more consistently successful than others.

THE CHEETAH

The cheetah is a small-headed but largish wild cat that is particularly agile and fast-moving (credited to be the fastest-moving land animal, achieving speeds of between 70 and 75 mph [112/120 km/h] in short bursts of up to 1,500ft (460m), with a potential acceleration from 0 to 68 mph [110 km/h] in 3 seconds. This implies very specific and relatively modern evolution, but in fact the cheetah is evolutionarily one of the oldest forms of wild cat (which is why it has only semi-retractable claws other than the dewclaws, and is least able to adapt to new environments). The cheetah may ultimately be related to a primeval species of dog. The name is from the Hindi *chita*, an adapted abbreviation of the Sanskrit *chitra-kaya* meaning 'bright body', a description

that would be disappointing to any cheetah that understood it, in that hunting cheetahs rely on their camouflage (notwithstanding the cheetah's mutative form of coloration involving merging spots).

The technical name of the cheetah is *Acinonyx jubatus*, and until recently it was regarded as a separate genus. *Acinonyx* means 'unmoving claw' and refers to the only semi-retractable claws; *jubatus* means 'maned'.

The animal's diet is mostly medium-sized to large deer and wildebeeste, hares and guinea-fowl – food it can catch in daylight, for it hunts by vision. Unusually, from ancient Egyptian times to the court of 1930s Emperor of Ethiopia Haile Selassie, cheetahs have been kept as fairly docile pets that were useful on hunting expeditions.

IN A FLAP

The inventor of the cat-flap entrance and exit – better known in the USA as a kitty door – is authoritatively said to have been the famous English mathematician and physicist Sir Isaac Newton (1642–1727).

BLAKE'S 'TYGER!'

ONE OF WILLIAM BLAKE'S most famous and most translated poems, 'The Tyger', is said by some to be an allegory of contemporary French Revolutionary zeal by a poet-artist whose early work included a volume entitled *The French Revolution* and who openly supported its ideals. Others have described the poem as no more than a rhetorical quest for the Creator of the Universe. But by including it in a collection called *Songs of Innocence and Experience* (1794), Blake evidently meant it it to be something more than merely rhetorical.

Tyger! Tyger! burning bright
In the forests of the night,
What immortal hand or eye
Could frame thy fearful symmetry?

In what distant deeps or skies
Burnt the fire of thine eyes?
On what wings dare he aspire?
What the hand dare seize the fire?

And what shoulder, and what art
Could twist the sinews of thy heart?
And when thy heart began to beat,
What dread hand? and what dread feet?

What the hammer? what the chain?
In what furnace was thy brain?
What the anvil? what dread grasp
Dare its deadly terrors clasp?

When the stars threw down their spears,
And watered heaven with their tears,
Did he smile his work to see?
Did he who made the Lamb make thee?

Tyger! Tyger! burning bright
In the forests of the night,
What immortal hand or eye
Dare frame thy fearful symmetry?

And it seems that the collective title *Songs ...* was also suggestive. Between 1913 and 2006 the poem was set to music no fewer than 56 times by 52 different composers, some using German or Russian translations, mostly for one or two voices and piano, but some for full four-part *a capella* chorus.

AN ADULT CAT HAS around 30 more bones in the body than the average adult human – but both cats and humans begin life with more bones than they end up with, because some bones fuse together as part of normal development. Nonetheless, cats are far more variable than humans in the total number of bones within them – a cat with a long tail has more bones than a cat with a short tail; a cat with extra toes correspondingly has extra bones there, too. The average cat's tail contains about 10% of the bones in its body. A cat's two collarbones are not attached to any other bone but surrounded by a muscular envelope, which enables it to squeeze its body through any gap wide enough for its head to pass through.

THE ANCIENT EGYPTIAN GODDESS BAST

The name of the ancient Egyptian cat (and fire and sun and war) goddess Bast is made up of two elements: *bas* (or *ubas*) 'devourer' and *-t* the feminine suffix. But although cats were mummified in her honour, she was depicted with the head of a lioness and regarded as the fierce protectress of her worshippers, defender of the pharaoh, and 'eye of Ra'. As time passed, the eminence of Bast in Egypt's Lower Kingdom diminished in favour of her cat goddess counterpart in the Upper Kingdom, Sekhmet, and when the two Kingdoms combined, Bast's name was changed slightly to Bastet, in which the addition of a second feminine suffix is thought to represent a diminutive. But this made her name the same as the ordinary Egyptian word for 'ointment-jar' (which was presumably of a shape and size not unlike a little cat's head), and Bast accordingly became associated also with scents and perfumes... and with the unguents of embalming. It is this that may explain why so many hundreds of thousands of cats were mummified in her name and buried next to their owners (and why for centuries she was held to be the assistant of Anubis, jackal-headed leader of human souls to the Underworld).

CATBIRDS

The North American catbird *Dumetella carolinensis* – a black-capped grey bird of the mockingbird family – is so named because its most common call is much like the 'miaow' of a cat, if perhaps a little squeakier. Australian catbirds (*Ailuroedus* spp), very different both in shape and coloration (predominantly green), are so called because they make a sound like a cat wailing.

A domestic cat can sprint briefly at about 31 miles per hour (50 km per hour).

CAT DIETETICS

Cats require specific nutrients not ordinarily available from a vegetarian diet, including vitamins A (retinol), B12, thiamine and niacin. Equally essential is the amino acid taurine: a lack or prolonged shortfall in a cat's diet can lead to retinal degradation and eventual blindness – cats alone among mammals seem to suffer this effect from that cause (dog foods rarely contain any taurine). Similarly deleterious symptoms arise in cats with a diet deficient in arachidonic acid. Meat is the sole major source of this and taurine for cats.

PRIDE OF THE PRIDE

Many baby boys are given a name that partly or wholly refers to the lion. Examples include:

Leo . . . . English	**Leon** . . . . English
Leão . . . . Portuguese	**Leon** . . . . .German
Lleó . . . . Catalan	**Leon** . . . . Irish
Llew . . . . Welsh	**Leon** . . . . .Jewish
Lew . . . . Polish	**Léon** . . . . French
Lev, Lyov . . . . Russian	**León** . . . . Spanish
Lev . . . . Bulgarian	**Leone** . . . . Italian
Leib . . . . Yiddish/Jewish	
[**Loewe, Löwe**. . . German surname]	**Leoš** . . . . .Czech
Lionel .English (a French diminutive)	**Leonard, Lennard** . . . . English
[**Lyall, Lyell**. . . . . English surnames]	[Germanic *leon* + *hard* 'lion hard']
	Léonard . . . . French
	Leonardo Italian/Spanish/Portuguese
Leonidas. . Greek [*leonidēs* 'lion-er']	**Lleonard** . . . . Catalan
Leonid . . . . Russian	**Lennart**. . . .Scandinavian Germanic
	Leonhard(t) . . . . .German
Leonzio . . . . Italian	[**Lehar** . . . . German surname]
[Latin *leontius* 'kin to the lion']	
Léonce . . . . French	**Leander** [Greek 'lion man'] . English
Leoncio . . . . Spanish	**Leandro** .Italian/Spanish/Portuguese
Leonti. . . . . .Russian	

SMALL INSECTIVOROUS ANIMALS much like today's pine martens gradually evolved from 60 million years ago to become the Miacidae and the Viverravidae. The Viverravidae gave rise first to Nimravidae, the 'false sabre-tooths' which were cat-like but not cats, and then the Aeluroidea, in which Proailurus may be described as the genuine 'first cat' (which is what its name means). Its successor, Pseudaelurus, thereafter evolved in two directions, resulting in both the Machairodontinae, the true sabre-tooth cats, and Schizailurus, the ancestor of the Felidae and all the cats of today. Meanwhile, genets, civets, mongooses and hyenas evolved separately though ultimately from the same source. It is surprising to think that today's big cats are the *latest* variants in this long evolutionary story.

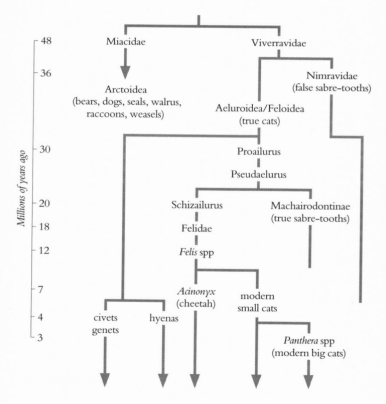

DARK VISION

Cats are often said to be able to see in the dark. They can't – not if it is genuinely dark and there is no light at all. But if there is any light, even if only starlight on a clear but moonless night, cats can use it far better than humans can. Because of a special absorptive surface (the tapetum lucidum) behind the retina of each eye which reflects and increases the light taken in by the photoreceptors, a cat needs only one sixth of the light that is the minimum a human needs in order to be able to navigate safely. From a human perspective, the cat is effectively magnifying the available light six times. The facility to do this relies on the fact that the cat's retina has proportionately more 'rod' cells than 'cone' cells on it, although a corresponding disadvantage is a reduction in the ability to distinguish colours in ordinary daylight. In tests, cats appear to be able to see only relatively moderate saturations of the colours purple, blue, green and yellow, all other shades seeming to them to be tones of grey. Nonetheless, another potential asset for cats is that the field of vision through the elliptical pupils of their eyes is about 185 degrees – some 5 degrees broader than that of humans at their best.

TELLING TAILS

As is neatly demonstrated by some of the names on the evolutionary chart opposite, one word-element that evidently refers to cats is *ailur-* or *aelur-*. It comes from the ancient Greek, in which 'cat' was *ailouros*, an expression that actually comprises two word-elements between them literally meaning 'tail driving one way and then the other'. The second constituent word-element is *ouros* 'tail', but the first element is derived from *aiolos* 'driving one way and then the other' – which is also the name for the Greek god of the winds, more usually in English and other languages spelled Aeolus.

It would seem that the ancient Greeks were not particularly fond of cats, nor cats of them, since association between both evidently caused the lashing of feline tails.

GOING TO A SHOW

At most cat shows you check in your cat and receive an envelope with an entry pass, the show numbers to be attached around the cat's neck, and a pen number. The attendant vet should then inspect your cat and look over its vaccination certificates. If all are in order, you will receive a 'vet slip'. You then proceed to the show hall and find the pen with your cat's pen number on it there. Settle your cat in the pen until the judging begins in the judging ring.

How do cats drink? A cat drinks using its tongue, on the surface of which (just as on the human tongue) are large numbers of little projections called papillae. But whereas the human tongue's papillae are fairly rounded, the cat's tongue's papillae are sharp enough to describe as serrated, not unlike rows of tiny teeth. This is useful when grooming – but it means that to drink, a cat has merely to push its tongue into the liquid and retract it again into its mouth, taking with it quantities of the liquid trapped between those rows of tiny teeth.

TIDDLES, OF PADDINGTON STATION

THIS STRAY SIX-WEEK-OLD KITTEN was adopted by the attendant at the ladies' lavatory at Paddington mainline railway station in London in 1970. The good-looking tabby-and-white cat very quickly became a celebrated fixture at the station, popular both with staff and daily passengers – to his own cost. For many of them regularly brought him quantities of food (particularly rabbit, steak, lambs' tongues, chicken livers and kidneys), which he evidently felt under some obligation to eat. After his fame spread through local then national newspaper reports, more parcels of food were delivered in the post every day (addressed simply to 'Tiddles, Paddington Station'). With much of his time thus occupied, he took little exercise. By 1982 he had became known to his admirers as the London Fat Cat Champion, and weighed in at a massive 13.6 kilograms (30 pounds), increasing over the following 12 months to 14.5 kilograms (32 pounds; over 2 stone). At that point his health was so poor that, to the sorrow of all who knew him, he had to be put to sleep.

KUCHING, MALAYSIA

The largest city on the island of Borneo, Kuching is the capital of the state of Sarawak in East Malaysia. Its population numbered 580,000 in 2006. Because *kuching* or *kucing* means 'cat' in Malay, local authorities have for at least a decade tried to popularize the place in the eyes of tourists by insisting that an alternative name for it is Cat City, and by erecting statues of cats here and there, and founding a celebrated Cat Museum. Yet the chances are that if the name has anything at all to do with cats, it is because of the former presence of many trees bearing mata kuching ('cat's eye') fruit. But since the city was originally founded by Indian coastal traders, an equally likely derivation for the name is the Hindi *cochin*, or 'port'. And it is just as possible that the city was named after the one well in the area in which, in the late nineteenth century, the water was guaranteed to be free from water-borne disease; it was in the Chinese quarter – the Chinese for 'the old well' is *ku-ching*.

L EO IS THE ZODIACAL CONSTELLATION held by the ancient Greeks to represent the Nemean Lion that featured as the subject of one of Hercules's mythical Labours. It lies between the other zodiacal constellations Cancer and Virgo, but is much easier to spot in the night sky as the prominent constellation immediately 'below' Ursa Major (the Great Bear, the Big Dipper) although technically there is the small and dim Leo Minor between them. Its zodiacal symbol is a florid version of the Greek letter *lambda*, which begins the ancient Greek name *Leōn*, but the constellation – sometimes only in part – has been known as the Lion since well before the Greeks, notably to the ancient Egyptians, the Babylonians, the ancient Persians and also to the Indo–Aryan invaders of Vedic India.

The name of the star Asad Australis (epsilon Leonis) is an abbreviation of *Ras al-Asad australis*, which is Arabic and Latin for 'head of the lion, south'. The name Algieba (gamma Leonis) also refers to the lion's head and is a version of Arabic *al jabhah*, 'the forehead', although it is located where the mane should be. The major star Regulus (alpha Leonis) is alternatively known as *Qalb al-Asad*, Arabic for 'heart of the lion'. Meanwhile, the name Denebola (beta Leonis) is a corruption of the Arabic *Deneb al-Asad*, 'tail of the lion'.

———————— THE SCAREDYCAT PLANT ————————

Plectranthus caninus (also known as *Coleus canina*) is a half-hardy plant with grey-green foliage and heads of pale blue flowers in summer. Attractive to humans, it gives off a strong aroma repellent to cats. For this reason, some householders grow the plant in pots that can be moved around the garden, protecting areas from feline attentions as and when needed. The plant prefers full sun but can bear light shade; it is easy to grow in any reasonable soil; and it can be overwintered in its pot in a frost-free location. Possibly because 'scaredy-cat' is a Britishism (US English: 'fraidy cat'), the plant is sometimes spelled 'scardycat' in the USA.

OFFENBACH'S CAT OPERETTAS

The French composer Jacques Offenbach (1819–80) wrote two operettas with cats in the title. The second is hardly ever remembered now and was called *Dick Whittington and His Cat*. It was Offenbach's one and only attempt to produce an English-style work not unlike something you'd find on a music-hall stage at Christmastime, using an English libretto by Henry B. Farnie. Dick Whittington is played by what used to be called a 'principal boy' – a lady soprano in drag. Most of the other characters are humorously exaggerated stereotypes. The cat instigates a love affair and saves a Pacific colony. On stage the action is fast, furious and funny, and the music is said to be up to Offenbach's best standards. But audiences in London in 1874 were not amused and hated it. Transferred to Paris – where for some reason it was entitled *Whittington, ou Le chat du diable*, although still sung partly in English and partly in translation by Charles Nuitter – French audiences loathed it even more. Apart from one single concert performance by Offenbach enthusiasts in London in the year 2000, it has now not been staged for more than 110 years and is rarely even listed among his works.

Offenbach's other 'cat' operetta is called *La chatte metamorphosée en femme* (1858), which remains much better known, and from which the music is also used as the basis for a ballet.

CAT CHROMOSOMES

A chromosome is a strand of DNA in a cell nucleus that carries the genetic material (the genes) inherited from an individual's parents and thus in number and arrangement the genes common to the individual's species. In humans there are 46 chromosomes per cell nucleus. In almost all cats the cell nuclei contain 38 chromosomes. Extraordinarily, however, there is a group of cats in which the cell nuclei contain 36 chromosomes instead – cats of the genus *Leopardus*, including the ocelot, Geoffroy's cat, the margay, the oncilla and the pampas cat – which makes them technically mutants. These 36-chromosome cats can nonetheless mate with 38-chromosome cats, although it rarely happens, and the resultant offspring then have 37 chromosomes per cell nucleus, the odd number of chromosomes causing them virtually always to be either females or sterile males.

A esop tells how the lion, the fox and the donkey all went hunting together having first agreed to share the spoils together afterwards. After a good day's sport, all the deer, boars, game birds and other creatures they had caught and killed were slung in a heap ready for allocation. The lion suggested to the donkey that he should make the distribution – and the donkey then carefully divided the heap into three equal portions before standing aside and requesting that the others choose their third. The lion, in a great rage, immediately leapt on the unfortunate donkey, and ate him. When he had finished, he politely invited the somewhat disconcerted fox to share out the spoils more appropriately. The fox quickly piled almost everything on one side, leaving only the tiniest and least interesting single morsel on the other side, which he made clear he intended was the portion meant for himself. The lion, evidently delighted, congratulated the fox and asked him who could possibly have taught him the art of dividing things up so sensibly and reasonably. 'Well,' said the fox, 'It was actually the donkey who taught me. I saw what happened to him.'

FUR COLORATION

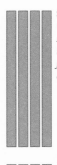

Self-colour
One single solid colour through the full length of each hair.

Dilute colour
One single solid colour but with areas of less pigment, appearing patchy.

Smoke
Undercoat much lighter (or white), visible when the cat walks.

Shaded
Undercoat and lower fur is white, visible when the cat walks or when the fur is parted by hand.

Tipped
Undercoat and most of the fur is white; all surface marking appears pale.

Ticked
Bands of coloration along hairs' length; coat contrasts provide the cat with good camouflage.

THE LEOPARD

THE LEOPARD is so called in most major languages of the world, but the name is actually from ancient Greek *leo-pardos*, 'lion-panther', via Latin. Now described technically as *Panthera pardus*, it is the smallest of the four 'big cats' of the *Panthera* genus – the others being the lion, the tiger and the jaguar – and lives mainly in sub-Saharan Africa, although there are small leopard communities in China, Indonesia, Malaysia and India. This represents a considerable reduction in total numbers – leopards were formerly distributed widely across Africa and Asia, and yet the leopard is currently regarded as the least environmentally threatened of its genus. A ferocious hunter, the leopard can run for short distances at 37 mph (60 km/h), leap more than 20 feet (6 metres) horizontally and jump up to 10 feet (3 metres) vertically. Its main diet comprises deer and antelope, monkeys and baboons, and other mammals of a similar size.

Since 1996, authorities have been trying to identify specific subspecies of leopard using DNA analysis. Ten subspecies have been identified, although two remain less acceptable in the eyes of some:

Panthera pardus adersi . . . . .Zanzibar leopard
Panthera pardus delacouri . . . . Indo–Chinese leopard
Panthera pardus fusca . . . . Indian leopard
Panthera pardus japonensis . . . . North Chinese leopard
Panthera pardus kotiya . . . . Sri Lankan leopard
Panthera pardus melas . . . . .Java leopard
Panthera pardus nimr . . . . Arabian leopard
Panthera pardus orientalis . . .Amur leopard of Korea, China & Eastern Russia
Panthera pardus pardus . . . . .African leopard
Panthera pardus saxicolor . . . . Persian/Iranian leopard

The snow leopard and the two clouded leopards are of different genera, although they are otherwise fairly closely related.

DEAD CAT BOUNCE

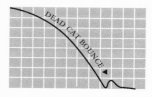

Dead cat bounce is a regrettable technical term used on the Wall Street Stock Market, dating from 1986. It means a slight recovery of share price after a precipitous fall – but probably too late and too little to effect any genuine revival. In other words, the cat remains dead, despite a little 'bounce'.

There are two major types of box- or cage-like carriers for transporting cats: top-loading and end-loading. In top-loading carriers, the entire top of the box or cage swings open for the cat to be gently dropped in, before the top is swung back and clipped shut. It is by far the more convenient, less stressful way to transport a cat unused to being handled, let alone transported. However, more popular among cat owners is the end-loading carrier – now generally made of plastic – in which a wide, transparent door is set in one end. Getting a cat into it relies on the cat's knowing what is intended . . . and not minding.

SHAKESPEARE'S 'CAT I' THE ADAGE'

SHAKESPEARE'S *Macbeth* is one of his most popular and most often translated tragedies. The plot centres on the murder by Macbeth of King Duncan in order that he should himself accede to the throne. But Macbeth is portrayed as a thoughtfully reluctant murderer by Shakespeare: Lady Macbeth has to urge him on to do the heinous deed, taunting him meanwhile not to be 'like the poor cat i' the adage', 'letting *I dare not* wait upon *I would*'. The adage – or popular saying – referred to is the one reported by John Heywood in his book of *Proverbs* (1546) some 60 years before Shakespeare here alluded to it: 'The cat would eate fishe, but would not wet her feete'. (In other words, the cat might want the result but is unwilling to go through what it takes to get it.)

JAGUAR CARS

JAGUAR CARS LTD was first so named in 1945, but derived as an offshoot of Swallow Sidecars Ltd (founded in 1922), a company that – as its name implies – concentrated on making sidecars for motorcycles. From 1934 the firm began also making motor vehicles and became known as SS Cars Ltd: hence the first SS Jaguar of 1935. The initials SS were dropped with the renaming of the company in 1945, partly because of all-too poignant possible Nazi associations.

The Jaguar used by Inspector Morse (played by John Thaw) in the world-syndicated TV series *Morse* is a 1960 Mark II 2.4-litre 'Regency red' model (registration mark 248 RPA), which was the smallest Jaguar saloon of its time, but could achieve a top speed of around 120 mph (195 km/h).

The Jaguar company changed hands quite a few times from the 1960s to the 1990s, but in June 2008 was bought (along with Land Rover) from Ford by Tata Motors of India.

The sea-bird known as the mew in English in fact has a name that corresponds to the word for 'sea-gull' in all other Germanic languages and Polish. Actually, the French word for 'sea-gull' is a diminutive form of the same word: *mouette* – but don't tell the French. Yet the name was of course originally meant to represent the call of the bird by referring it to the sound of a young cat. As a sort of extension of this, the sea-bird now known in German, Dutch and Swedish as the 'three-toed mew' (*Rissa tridactyla*) was formerly known in English as the cattiwake, but is listed in current field guides as the kittiwake, again because of its supposedly feline cry.

CATS & THEIR TEETH

At birth, kittens have no teeth at all. However, between the third and sixth weeks of a kitten's life, its milk (deciduous) teeth appear – incisors and canines first, followed by lower premolars and upper premolars – a total of 26 teeth. It takes another three to six months before the second and permanent dentition appears, replacing the kitten's deciduous teeth one-for-one. After the additional eruption of the adult molars, the total number of teeth is 30 (12 incisors, 4 canines, 10 premolars, and 4 molars). Because cats have evolved essentially as carnivores, the teeth described as 'carnassial' are particularly well developed: these are the four teeth (the fourth upper premolar and the first lower molar on each side) that slice up meat as the jaws close vertically. In some other mammals these teeth have evolved in a different way to fulfil a different purpose: those of bears and pandas, for example, have evolved to be able to grind vegetable matter in a much more rotatory manner. A lion, on the other hand, not only has particularly prominent carnassial teeth but strong and pointed incisors and enlarged canines for transfixing prey, together with exaggerated zygomatic arches – the cheekbones – to which super-powerful jaw muscles are attached for chewing and grinding.

FREYA'S CATS

Freya (or Freyja), the Norse goddess of love, beauty and fertility, rode through the sky in a chariot pulled by two blue cats that had been presented to her as kittens by the thunder-and-lightning god Thor. The cats had, from an early age, been accustomed to flying. Their father – who asked Thor to find his kittens a good home – apparently had the power of flight. It was in honour of Freya that the Vikings used to give young couples cats when they married and set up home together: the cats would not only catch and kill mice but keep the young wives company while their husbands went a-viking in summer.

THE INTERNATIONAL TIGER

Called a 'tiger' in most major languages of the world (see below), the tiger is
the large Asian cat *Panthera tigris* 'proverbial for its ferocity and cunning' – in
Middle English it is *tygre*, from Latin/Greek *tigris*, originally from Old Persian
meaning something corresponding to 'arrow-like' and etymologically identical
with the river-name Tigris.

French	*tigre*	English	*tiger*
Italian	*tigre*	German	*Tiger*
Spanish	*tigre*	Dutch	*tijger*
Portuguese	*tigre*	Swedish	*tiger*
modern Greek	*tígrē*	Danish	*Tiger*
Basque	*tigre*	Norwegian	*tiger*
		Icelandic	*tigur*
Latvian	*tīgeris*	Albanian	*tigër*
Lithuanian	*tigras*	Czech	*tiger*
Polish	*tygrys*	Bulgarian	*tiger*
Hungarian	*tigris*	Serbo-Croat	*tigar*
		Russian	*tigr*
Welsh	*teigr*	Estonian	*tiiger*
Scottish/Irish	*tíogar*	Finnish	*tiikeri*

In North America, the term 'tiger' is also used in relation to the jaguar and
the cougar/puma/panther/painter (just as in South Africa the term may
alternatively be used of the leopard). Strangely, although 'tiger' is derived from
Old Persian, modern Persian (Farsi) uses the word *babr* for the animal. Tiger
in Arabic is *nimr*; in Hebrew, *namer*; in Chinese, *hu*; and in Turkish, *kaplan*.

MAN'S SECOND-BEST FRIEND

Cats have been 'domesticated' for
half the time dogs have been.

DOMESTIC CATS CAN HEAR SOUNDS at both lower and higher pitches/
frequencies than humans – especially higher. In fact, their hearing range is
wider than that of many other animals, as measured in Hertz:

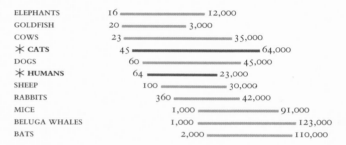

ELEPHANTS	16 ———————— 12,000	
GOLDFISH	20 ———— 3,000	
COWS	23 ——————————— 35,000	
✳ CATS	45 ——————————————— 64,000	
DOGS	60 ———————————— 45,000	
✳ HUMANS	64 ————————— 23,000	
SHEEP	100 ————————— 30,000	
RABBITS	360 ——————————— 42,000	
MICE	1,000 ——————————————— 91,000	
BELUGA WHALES	1,000 ——————————————— 123,000	
BATS	2,000 ——————————————— 110,000	

Moreover, a cat has ears that are designed not only for extraordinary mobility
– each ear can be independently turned through 180 degrees – but also for
drawing sound in towards the eardrum. This means that a cat hears things faster
(and can therefore react faster) than most other animals, including dogs, and can
locate where sounds are coming from with greater precision. Unfortunately,
that super-sensitivity also means that in a household that is constantly filled
with high-volume sounds a cat may, over time, go deaf.

—— YURI KUKLACHEV'S CAT THEATRE, MOSCOW ——

Cat trainer, clown and Cat Theatre proprietor Yuri Kuklachev insists that
cats *cannot* be trained – they do only what they want to do – and the trick is
to try to get them to want to do what you want them to do. The result is that in
the popular shows he puts on for Moscow family audiences, one or two of the
140 or so cats in his troupe invariably decide to do something different from
the script. But such potential disasters tend just to add to the fun. Acts include

versions of *The Nutcracker* and *Cats From Outer Space*;
some involve breathtaking feline agility and athleti-
cism, and are interspersed with children's novelty acts
organized by other members of Kuklachev's family.
A degree of audience participation is expected. Many
of the cats are former strays, but Kuklachev reckons
to be able to communicate with any cat, and does so
very successfully. The Cat Theatre toured the US in
2005 and 2006-7, the only disappointment being
how often the press referred to the theatre as a 'circus'.

CATS HAVE EVOLVED to have tremendously strong forearms, both for hanging on to prey they have chased and caught, and for climbing up tall trees (and, if sensible enough, for climbing back down again). Obtaining this extra strength has, however, required some structural alteration in the bones of the forearm in comparison with the forearm bones of a human. Whereas a human can stretch the arms out in front and rotate the forearms to show palms up or palms down, cats have no such rotational facility – their strength comes mainly from the greatly increased rigidity of the elbows and wrists: for them it is the equivalent of palms down only.

From a human perspective, and in technical terms, cats have developed an elongated ulna that is firmly locked to the radius – the scapho-lunar and hamate bones of the wrist are fused, forming a single bone and the centrale has disappeared altogether. These are all measures evidently designed to *prevent* rotation.

SHOW JUDGING

When the judging at a cat show begins, cats are brought one by one from the holding pens to the empty pens at the judging ring. You may bring your cat yourself, and hand it to a steward there, or you may ask the steward to take your cat from the holding pen to the ring. The judge will examine your cat very carefully, and simultaneously or immediately afterwards write out a report. If you are on hand while the judging takes place, be careful not to address the judge, for any attempt at even light conversation might be interpreted as interference, if nothing worse. The judge's report, with any nomination for a rosette, ribbon or other form of award, is passed on to the show secretariat, members of which will then relay the information to you and other exhibitors, and distribute any awards won. If your cat is best in its class, you will also probably be told at this point that your cat is one of the Best In Show nominees, the final element of the judging, representing the show's culmination.

The ribbon and rosette colours awarded are usually those decreed by the national or regional cat show authority (such as the UK's GCCF). Typical colours however, are those set by the Cat Fanciers' Association (CFA) in the USA:

First place in class	*dark blue*
Second place in class	*red*
Third place in class	*yellow*
Best of colour class	*black*
Championship winner	*red, white & blue*
Premier winner	*red, white & blue*
Best of breed/division	*brown*
Household pet merit award	*red & white*

Dusty, a tabby in Texas, currently holds the record for having given birth to the most kittens during a lifetime. In June 1952 she had her last litter at the age of 18, and the final count was 420.

Some 35 years later, in May 1987, a cat living in Staffordshire, central England, called Litty – who had already given birth to 216 kittens – gave birth to her last litter of two kittens at the grand old age of 30. She is the oldest cat mother on record.

——————— OSCAR AKA UNSINKABLE SAM ———————

Oscar was possibly the unluckiest – or the luckiest – ship's cat there has ever been. He began as the pet of an unknown crewman on the German battleship *Bismarck* during World War II, and was on board when it was sunk on its first mission in May 1941. Floating on wreckage, the little black-and-white cat was picked up by the British destroyer HMS *Cossack* and, under the name Oscar, became its ship's cat for a few months on convoy duty in the Mediterranean and the North Atlantic. In October 1941, *Cossack* was in turn torpedoed off Gibraltar, and the surviving crew – including Oscar – were taken to Gibraltar, where he became known as Unsinkable Sam, and where, because of the spreading fame of his good luck, the authorities quickly sought to find him another ship. The aircraft carrier HMS *Ark Royal* was in port, and Oscar/Sam duly joined it. Within days, however, the *Ark Royal*, too, was terminally damaged by enemy action, and the crew – with the cat – were again returned to Gibraltar. Oscar/Sam's seagoing days were now deemed to be over, and after a short stint as resident cat in the Governor of Gibraltar's office, he retired in 1944 to a seamen's mission home in Belfast, Northern Ireland, where, after 11 apparently contented landlubberly years, he passed away.

There is a pastel portrait (*Oscar, the Bismarck's Cat*) by artist Georgina Shaw-Baker in London's Greenwich National Maritime Museum.

——————— THE LEONID METEOR SHOWER ———————

From the point of view of an observer on Earth, the constellation Leo (the zodiacal Lion) is the apparent source of the annual shower of meteors – fragments of space dust – left by the comet Tempel-Tuttle through which the orbit of the Earth takes it in mid-November. These meteors are known therefore as the Leonids. During the mid-nineteenth century it was noted that the Leonids regularly rise and fall in intensity over a period of 33 years. The 1966 Leonid meteor shower was one of the heaviest meteor showers ever recorded; the eagerly anticipated shower of 1999 was, however, disappointing.

'You see, wire telegraph is a kind of a very, very long cat. You pull his tail in New York and his head is meowing in Los Angeles. Do you understand this? And radio operates exactly the same way: you send signals here, they receive them there. The only difference is that there is no cat.'

ALBERT EINSTEIN, *when asked to describe radio*

——————— CAT'S ELBOW, GERMANY ———————

KATZENELNBOGEN is a small city with an originally medieval castle overlooking the River Lahn in western Germany. Its apparently modern German name – in English, it translates as 'Cat's elbow' – is deceptive, however, for the name actually derives from what the Romans called the area a century or so into the first millennium AD. They called it after the names of the two mountain tribes who lived locally: the Chatti and the Meliboci, and over the centuries since, *Chatti-Meliboci* has through some folk-etymology been assimilated to Katzenelnbogen.

HERALDIC LIONS

Lions that belong to ancient and traditional coats of arms tend to be portrayed in certain stylized positions. Eagles, bears, leopards, unicorns, griffons and one or two other creatures may well be seen in some of these same heraldic poses, but lions have probably the greatest repertoire.

lion rampant

lion salient

lion passant

lion statant

lion séjant

lion couchant

THE CAT'S CLAW VINE

CAT'S CLAW (*Uncaria tomentosa*) is a vine that grows mainly in South America and parts of Asia; the inner bark and root contain substances with valuable medicinal properties. Both its common name and the first part of its scientific name refer, however, to the claw-like thorns at the bottom of each leaf, which act as bases to enable the vine to climb up host trees sometimes to 100 feet (30 metres). Its active chemical constituents – mainly alkaloids and tannins – may be used to treat hypertension, control cholesterol, relieve gastrointestinal disorders, reduce inflammation, slow the advance of some forms of cancer, and (in combination with the drug AZT) assist in the treatment of AIDS. It is not surprising then that the cat's claw (*una de gato*) is a protected species in Peru.

'WHAT'S NEW, PUSSYCAT?'

Title song, by Burt Bacharach and Hal David and sung by Tom Jones, of the movie of the same name (1965) starring Peter Sellers, Peter O'Toole and Romy Schneider, directed by Clive Donner and Richard Talmadge, original screenplay by Woody Allen. Also starring were Capucine, Ursula Andress, Paula Prentiss and Woody Allen, and there were cameo appearances by Richard Burton and chanteuse Françoise Hardy. The title is apparently a greeting used frequently and famously at the time by Warren Beatty either to his girlfriends and potential girlfriends or (according to a different source) to all callers over the telephone, and thus actually has nothing to do with real cats. The original intention was that Beatty would be the primary star of the film, but the then unknown Woody Allen's script upgraded a different role to become the hero's, and Beatty, apparently in high dudgeon, dropped out – and refused ever again thereafter to work with Woody Allen.

PAWS FOR THOUGHT

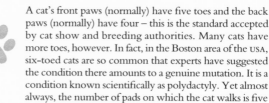

A cat's front paws (normally) have five toes and the back paws (normally) have four – this is the standard accepted by cat show and breeding authorities. Many cats have more toes, however. In fact, in the Boston area of the USA, six-toed cats are so common that experts have suggested the condition there amounts to a genuine mutation. It is a condition known scientifically as polydactyly. Yet almost always, the number of pads on which the cat walks is five per paw – the larger metacarpal pad and four smaller pads (as shown stylized here). So the paw prints of fore and hind feet are virtually the same, and there is (usually) no indication of how many toes the cat has.

AND KASPAR MAKES FOURTEEN

LONDON'S SAVOY HOTEL has a famous restaurant known as the Savoy Grill at which tradition forbids dinner parties numbering 13; this rule follows a tragedy in 1898 when a guest in a party of 13 laughed off the number's unluckiness, and shortly afterwards was shot dead. For some years at the beginning of the twentieth century a member of staff made up a fourteenth. Then, in the mid-1920s a sculpture was commissioned from Basil Ionides, and Kaspar the Cat was born. Shiny and blackish-brown, and described as wood or alabaster, Kaspar has ever since attended as the fourteenth of parties of 13, and been solemnly served with every course of the meal. And it is claimed that no one else has been shot dead afterwards.

HUMAN RELATIONSHIPS

'As a cat owner, I know the truth of the old joke where the dog says to himself: "He feeds me, he strokes me, he must be God." The cat says: "He feeds me, he strokes me, I must be God." '
HELEN WOMACK, *The Independent*, 27 April 1999

THE MATAGOT

According to some oral traditions of southern France, a *matagot* (or *mandagot*) is a spirit creature that takes a rather fuzzy and ill-defined form sometimes taken to be that of a cat, but equally sometimes regarded as in the shape of a dog, fox, rat, or even cow. Such spirit beings are mostly malevolent, but this variant type may bring wealth to a household if it is fed well enough. By tradition, a wealth-conveying *matagot* has first to be lured by an offering of a fresh, plump chicken, and then must be carried home by the householder, who must never once look back. Once in the home, the cat must be given the first mouthful of food and drink at every meal – the *matagot* then will repay the householder one solid gold coin per day (although under present institutions in most countries today, this sort of regular income would demand a degree of essential money laundering). It is depressingly likely that this unusual form of the *matagot* is derived at least partly through linguistic confusion, and has much to do with the local dialectal word *magot*, which means 'treasure'.

The top ten countries in the world by total population
of domestic cats in 2006 were:

1. **USA** . . . . *76.43 million*	6. **Italy** . . . . *9.4 million*
2. **China** . . . . *53.1 million*	7. **UK** . . . . *7.7 million*
3. **Russia** . . . . *12.7 million*	8. **Ukraine** . . . . *7.35 million*
4. **Brazil** . . . . *12.466 million*	9. **Japan** . . . . *7.3 million*
5. **France** . . . . *9.6 million*	10. **Germany** . . . . *6.7 million*

But if these populations were compared with the total human population of
the time and place, a different concept of cat popularity might emerge:

1. **USA** . . . . . *1 cat per 3.925 humans*	6. **Russia** . . . *1 cat per 11.26 humans*
2. **Italy** . . . . . *1 cat per 6.184 humans*	7. **Germany** . . *1 cat per 12.3 humans*
3. **Ukraine** . . *1 cat per 6.395 humans*	8. **Brazil** . . . . *1 cat per 14.78 humans*
4. **France** . . . *1 cat per 6.536 humans*	9. **Japan** . . . . *1 cat per 17.53 humans*
5. **UK** . . . . *1 cat per 7.79 humans*	10. **China** . . . . *1 cat per 24.48 humans*

And in terms of the ratio of cat numbers to human numbers, it should
perhaps also be noted that in Europe it is the Republic of Ireland that has by
far the highest tally: 1 cat per 4.44 humans in 2007.

———————— THE LYNX ————————

This medium-sized wild cat was, until the very end of the twentieth century, classified in its own genus, *Lynx*, but has since come to be regarded as an extension of the *Felis* genus of smaller cats (including the domestic cat). Nonetheless, under its older *Lynx* denomination, there were held to be four separate species: *Lynx lynx* (the Eurasian lynx), *L. canadensis*, *L. pardinus* (the Iberian lynx) and *L. rufus* (the bobcat). Major habitats are northern Europe (Scandinavia, Estonia, Poland, northern Russia), Romania, the Iberian peninsula, and Canada and northern USA – anywhere there are montane forests with heavy undergrowth and flowing water, no matter how cold; pockets are also resident in some Himalayan areas. The main diet of the lynx is rabbits and hares where there is an abundance of them (in Canada and the Iberian peninsula, for example), and larger animals such as roe and red deer, where they are more plentiful (as in Poland and Russia).

The name 'lynx' is common to many European languages (notably those deriving from Latin) but is cognate with the English word *light* (referring apparently to its bright eyes), as is the name for the animal in other European languages, such as German, where it is known as *Luchs*, and in Lithuanian as *lušis*.

Note that the caracal, although sometimes referred to as the African or Persian lynx, is not directly related and is of its own genus, *Caracal*.

The tortoiseshell cat – or 'tortie' – was first so called in English and as late as in 1782. Since then, the description has been translated pretty well directly into most other languages (thus *Schildpattkatze* in German, and *chat marqué en écaille de tortue* in French), although in the us, tortoiseshell cats may alternatively be described as calimanco or clouded tiger cats, and a tortie with a predominantly white coat may be described as calico. Almost all torties are (for genetic reasons) female – and are known for being distinctly independent-minded.

CAT ACCESSORIES

The list of available accessories for domestic cats is impressively long – but not as long as the list of accessories for dogs. Yet the standard accessories in most cat-owning households are merely:

* bowls for water and food
* cat carrier, for any sudden necessity to visit the vet
* supply of tablets against fleas, worms or other minor infestations
* grooming aids if the cat is a show cat (or particularly scruffy)

Nonetheless, a number of cat care companies advertise a selection of further, rather more eclectic accessories, some of which should perhaps be more popular than they are. These include:

* a cat bed or padded basket
* a cat collar (some of which now have a weak link that snaps in an emergency; others of which come in designer colours or decoration) with an ID tag displaying name, address and any chip reference
* a cat scratching-post
* cat toys (some part-chewable or even part-edible; many in the shape of mice or fluffy birds)
* cat 'treats' (many edible, but including items such as catnip cushions)
* the feline equivalent of a canine kennel (sometimes called a 'cat cabin')

THE OMNISCIENT CAT

'I have studied many philosophers and many cats. The wisdom of cats is infinitely superior.'
HIPPOLYTE TAINE (1825–96), *French historian & literary critic*

Rather than suggest that one human year is seven 'cat years', many people say that the first two human years should count as 25 cat years, and each human year thereafter is equivalent to four cat years.

PUMA SPORTS SHOES

THE PUMA SPORTS SHOE (and sports equipment) company began in 1948, when Rudolf Dassler left his brother Adolf ('Adi') Dassler and their joint company, and moved across to the other side of the River Aurach to found the Puma Schuhfabrik Rudolf Dassler in Herzogenaurach, Germany. His factory made sports shoes, especially concentrating on the new invention of the screw stud for soccer boots (1949/50), which became the company's main seller and promoted product. (In the meantime, Adi Dassler changed the name of the brothers' former company to 'adidas', which has ever since been a strong, if not dominant, rival.) By 1952, however, the Puma company's athletics shoes, mostly for track sprinters, were of equal promotional value, with tennis shoes becoming so, too. And indeed between the 1950s and the 2000s, hardly a major annual sporting event in the world was not won at one time or another by someone using Puma footwear. By the 1990s Puma was sponsoring football teams and committing itself to backing international events (such as the Red Bull Air Race and the World Rally Championship). From the mid-1990s the company was opening subsidiary companies around the world, including those in the USA, Italy, Chile and Romania.

WHISKERY ANTENNAE

A cat (usually) has three whiskers in four rows on each side of its face, making a total of 24 whiskers. Each whisker is more than twice as thick as an ordinary hair, and implanted three times deeper, too, with a large number of nerve endings and a rich blood supply, making each whisker very sensitive to air movement and to touch. In fact, so sensitive are the whiskers that they give the cat all kinds of information about the nearby environment without necessarily involving the sense of touch at all. But when touch is involved, the cat's ability to move the upper two rows of whiskers on each side of the face independently of the bottom two mean that it can judge the shape and relative distance of things close up. It also means that if a cat is eating from a bowl that is so narrow that the whiskers are always touching the sides, the cat may be deterred from using the bowl at all, no matter how much he likes what's in it.

THE INTERNATIONAL CAT

THE WORD 'CAT' seems to be earlier than Indo-European in derivation, since it occurs in an equivalent form in some of the languages akin through what is known as the Nostratic relationship (such as Hebrew, Finnish and Turkish):

English	*cat, kit(ten)*	Portuguese	*gato*
Welsh	*cath*	modern Greek	*gáta*
Basque	*catu*	Turkish	*kedi*
French	*chat*	Icelandic	*köttur*
German	*Katze*	Russian	*kot, koshka*
Dutch	*kat*	Polish	*kot(a)*
Swedish	*katt*	Czech	*kočka*
Danish	*Katt*	Bulgarian	*kotka*
Norwegian	*katt*	Estonian	*kass*
Lithuanian	*katè*	Finnish	*kissa*
Hebrew	*khatul*	Arabic	*qitt(a)*
Italian	*gatto*	Malay	*kucing*
Spanish	*gato*	Latvian	*kakis*

WORDS FOR 'CAT' in a number of other languages (one or two of them Indo-European) seem – with unexpected consistency – to begin with 'm-', although whether this is connected in some way with the sound a cat makes (as in English, *miaow*), or whether these words have any common derivation, is unknown.

Chinese	*mao*	Albanian	*mica*
Hungarian	*macska*	Thai	*mairo*
Serbo-Croat	*mačka*	Sanskrit	*marjari*

OTHER LANGUAGES are quite different, their words for cat possibly deriving from some dialectal description or nickname:

Romanian	*pisica*	Hindi	*billī*
Swahili	*paka*	Persian/Farsi	*gorbeh*
Japanese	*néko*		

NB. It is interesting that neither ancient Greek (*ailouros* 'tail driving one way and then the other') nor classical Latin (*feles* 'breeder', 'good producer') used the more historical term for 'cat', and yet the word was in the dialectal vocabulary of both and derivative languages of both have reverted to it.

A T BIRTH, the typical kitten weighs a mere 85 grams (3 ounces) but over the next 18 months will grow to an average weight of 3.2 to 4 kilograms (7 to 9 pounds) if male, and 2.75 to 3.6 kilograms (6 to 8 pounds) if female, if fed properly and if the cat exercises outdoors but lives mainly indoors. Normally, housecats do not overeat, but when not allowed to exercise outdoors, cosseted indoors, and constantly presented with fresh and appetizing food, they may over-indulge – and grow fat (although many serious internal disorders may give rise to the same effect).

The heaviest cat ever formally recorded – a male cat called Himmy, in Australia – weighed in at a massive 21.3 kilograms (just under 47 pounds)... and died of respiratory failure at the age of ten in 1986.

——————— ARE CATS INTELLIGENT? ———————

A cat's IQ – a measure of the ability to put into practice what has been learned and is remembered – is reckoned to be second in the animal kingdom only to that of monkeys and the higher apes. Cats are certainly able to think constructively and purposefully, using what they have learned mainly from their mothers but also from surrounding humans to solve problems and adapt to circumstances that are changing. It has been further shown in tests that a cat's memory of an event can be retained without reinforcement or repetition for up to 16 hours (or until the cat falls asleep), which is actually better than most monkeys. Without reinforcement or repetition, a dog's memory of an event lasts for no more than 5 minutes.

——————— SCHRÖDINGER'S CAT ———————

Schrödinger's cat is the name of a 'thought experiment' devised by the Austrian physicist Erwin Schrödinger in 1935 in response to what he saw as an anomaly in one of the contemporary theories of quantum mechanics (the 'Copenhagen interpretation') in the way it might be applied to everyday surroundings. Whereas in ordinary thinking, for example, a cat might be held to remain alive or to be dead following a specific but random event, Schrödinger pointed out that according to the Copenhagen interpretation, the cat might under certain circumstances be both alive *and* dead at a particular moment, but only while unobserved. Albert Einstein himself wrote to congratulate Schrödinger on what he deemed to be an insightful summary of a genuine scientific problem that centres on how the observation or measurement of an event may be so significant that the final outcome does not exist and cannot be recorded until that particular observation or measurement is made.

THE MANEKI NEKO

THIS LUCKY 'beckoning cat' figurine is generally made of ceramic or other earthenware material, papier-mâché or varnished wood, and stands prominently at or close to the main door of many Japanese shops. The cat is 'beckoning' because it has one or both paws raised alongside its head. If the paw raised is its left, the cat is beckoning in welcome to customers and browsers, assuring them of a satisfactory visit. If the paw raised is its right, the cat is beckoning towards the spirit of good fortune and prosperity and incidentally assuring visitors that the shop is a place from which good fortune and prosperity may spring. This type of the cat figurine is often described outside Japan as the 'lucky cat' or the 'money cat' (and is available in Europe, North America and Australasia in the somewhat debased form of small lucky charms and money-boxes).

BEST IN SHOW

For those who are still competing, those who are judging, and those who are spectating with no personal interest in the outcome, the judging of the Best in Show at a cat show is usually the highlight of the day. After all the nominations have been listed and reviewed, the nominated cats are brought before the panel of judges for them to vote for the cat of their choice. Discussion ensues and – perhaps after a wait that may be nerve-wracking for the owners – a decision is made on the best cat. The winning cat's number is chalked up on a board, which is rotated for all to see. A trophy specific to the event may be presented.

CATS DOWN UNDER

Although the USA has for many years had the largest total number of cats of any country in the world, and although the number of cats there has increased dramatically over the past decade, the chances are that New Zealand remains the country that, since 1999, has the greatest number of cats in relation to the human population. Research to this effect was commissioned by a pet food company and showed in addition that:

✦ only 10% of cats in households were purebred (pedigree) cats; the vast majority were of mixed breed
✦ people obtained their cats mainly (37%) through friends; some 14% took on a cat from the Society for the Prevention of Cruelty to Animals.

A cat named Towser is described in *The Guinness Book of Records* as having in her working life caught and killed no fewer than 28,899 mice. Mice are, of course, a real pest in any place that uses grain – and Towser lived in the Glenturret Distillery near Crieff, in Scotland (where, among other brands, they produce The Famous Grouse whisky). Even so, a total of 28,899 over, let's say, 23 years (for Towser retired at the grand old age of 24) would require the despatch of 3.44 mice per day, every day, without a break, for all those years. A bronze statue of the cat stands on a roughish plinth at The Famous Grouse Experience Visitors' Centre at Glenturret – but the memorial plaque beneath it fails to mention the local rumour that Towser's remarkable success was based partly on a daily dram of The Famous Grouse in her saucer of milk.

───────────── THE ASTRAL LYNX ─────────────

LYNX is the name of a small and ill-defined constellation in the northern night sky visible 'to the right of' Ursa Major/the Big Dipper (i.e. parallel to and outside Ursa Major's 'the Pointers'). The constellation was 'invented' in the late seventeenth century by Johannes Hevelius, also known as Johann Hewelke/ Höwelcke or Jan Heweliusz, a Polish-Lithuanian mayor of the Baltic city-port of Danzig/Gdansk, a master brewer and an astronomer sometimes called 'the father of lunar topography', and as a leading European astronomer also a friend of Edmund Halley (of Halley's Comet) and a member of the (British) Royal Society. It should be said that Hevelius's own depiction of the animal lynx after which he named the constellation – as represented on his star map – looks horribly unlike the now-familiar member of the cat family and instead closely resembles a grumpy sheep. It was also Hevelius who similarly added (the nearby) Leo Minor to star charts and described the brightest of its generally very dim stars as *praecipua*, 'primary', from a century later taken to be its proper name (although it is otherwise known simply as '46').

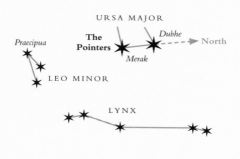

'I had been told that the training procedure with cats was difficult.
It's not. Mine had me trained in two days.'
BILL DANA, *US comedian, actor & screenwriter*

—————— CATFORD, LONDON ——————

CATFORD is a large urban residential area of south-east London, England, at the centre of the modern Borough of Lewisham. However, when it was named in the middle of the thirteenth century it was no more than a rather insignificant river crossing (a ford) some 6 miles/10 kilometres away from a much smaller London and out in the countryside, where an unusual number of wild cats used to gather to watch geese, ducks and other farm animals make their way across the Ravens' Burn (now known as the River Ravensbourne) on their way to the local town markets in the county of Kent. Perhaps Catford's main claim to fame today is a well-attended beer festival held annually under the auspices of the Campaign for Real Ale (CAMRA) in its art-deco-style Broadway Theatre.

—————— THE SYMBOLIC TIGER ——————

The tiger is the third animal in the Chinese zodiac (after the rat and the ox), and in that context is associated with good fortune, power and royalty, partly because whereas in the West the lion is 'the king of beasts', in the Far East it is the tiger that is given that distinction.

The next Year of the Tiger begins in what in the West is AD 2010. (Previous Years of the Tiger began in 1998, 1974, 1962, 1950, 1938, 1926 and 1914.) People born in such years are thought to be particularly sensitive, both in being aware of and sympathetic to the feelings of others and in occasionally taking offence where none was intended. Tiger people tend to dislike obeying orders, and when their minds are made up, they can be tigerishly determined in pursuit of their goals. In personal relationships, Tigers are most compatible with Dragons, Horses and Dogs.

The tiger was often used in China as an emblem or carving in official seals and staffs or tokens of office. Such tokens of office were in former centuries often made in two halves (called 'tiger tallies'), and possession of both halves symbolized and guaranteed genuineness. The association with good fortune is partly folk etymological – the pronunciation of *hu* in many dialects is the same as of *fu*, 'blessing', 'earned success', 'earned pre-eminence' – as in the name of the martial art kung fu (*gung fu*), or 'earned success over hard labour'.

LEFT, LEFT, RIGHT, RIGHT

Like only camels and giraffes among other four-legged animals, cats do not use a treading pattern involving left and right legs alternately. Instead, the paws touch the ground in an order that repeats the sequence:

left front paw ✳ *left rear paw* ✳ *right front paw* ✳ *right rear paw*

While the cat is walking unfussedly forwards, the pattern is completed so smoothly and rhythmically – in what to humans may seem like half-steps, but which is often more than one paw on the ground simultaneously – there is no evident awkwardness in the movement, and no lurching from side to side as you might expect.

'LEAVE MY KITTEN ALONE'

There can't be many Beatles' numbers that are comparatively unknown even to their fans, but 'Leave My Kitten Alone' is perhaps one. It was recorded by the band in 1964 and intended for inclusion on the *Beatles For Sale* album, but the final mix was apparently deemed unacceptable, and the track only eventually appeared on the album *Anthology 1* (disc 2). The number was not an original Beatles song anyway.

A bouncy twelve-bar blues with somewhat pugnacious lyrics, it was written by Little Willie John, Titus Turner and James McDougal, and features the warning-off of an interloper (addressed as 'big fat bulldog') for paying too much attention to the object of the lead singer's adoration, 'my kitten'. The lead singer on this occasion was John Lennon. Elvis Costello has since recorded the title on the album *Kojak Variety* (1995).

THE CAT-FACED SPIDER

THE CAT-FACED SPIDER (*Araneus gemmoides*), sometimes called just the cat spider but more properly known as the western plains orbweaver, is one of the largest spiders in south-western and central Canada and in the north-western and central USA. Its bite is mildly venomous to humans, but it tends to avoid confrontation, possibly because when it does not live out in the pine forests or among rough rocks, one of its other main chosen habitats is the outside of human residences and outbuildings, in eaves and lighting fitments and under sills and overhangs. It is called the cat-faced spider because the round-bodied female has two triangular raised areas on its abdomen that resemble cats' ears close to two dark roundish indentations that resemble eyes.

FELIX THE CAT

Felix The Cat began in a short (silent) animation movie called *Feline Follies*, which was directed by Otto Messmer and produced by Pat Sullivan in the early 1900s before becoming a cartoon strip (from 1923) drawn primarily by Joe Oriolo and syndicated by King Features worldwide. Felix was Charles Lindbergh's mascot on his historic transatlantic flight (1927) and the model used for experimental TV broadcasting by RCA from 1928. In animated form he remains popular on TV today.

The connection between the name Felix and the word *feline*, however, has, in English, been made for at least three centuries. Linguistically, it goes right back to the original Latin. In classical Latin, the word for 'cat' was *feles* (or *felis*), which was introduced as a slang term applied at first strictly to wild cats and which actually meant 'breeder' or 'good producer'. The relevant adjective derived from it was *felinis*, or 'feline' – although this word remained slang during Classical times and became standard usage only later as the ordinary Latin for 'cat' was reverting back to the more historical *catta* (or *cattus*). Throughout the whole period, however, the Latin word *felix* was virtually an extension of *felis*, 'good producer', apprehended as meaning 'producer of good', thus 'source of good luck'. The result was *felicitas*, 'felicity' (another modern personal name).

The connection also accounts for the name of the proprietary cat food brand Felix (part of the Nestlé Purina Petcare UK group).

FURRY WITCH

The *cat sidh* (sometimes incorrectly spelled *caith sith*) is a 'magic cat' said in Scotland to be as large as a dog, with a white spot on its breast, and to be a transformed witch. Actually, the origin of the *cat sidh* is almost certainly what is now known as the Kellas cat – a large black hybrid between feral domestic cats and Scottish wild cats. Specimens of these unusual animals were given thorough scientific examination during the 1980s.

TIGER ON THE GEIGER

A radioactive cat has eighteen half-lives.

The American Veterinary Medical Association noted that, in 2007:

HOUSEHOLDS	CATS	DOGS
❀ *percentage of households owning:*	32.4	37.2
❀ *total number of households owning:*	37,460,000	43,021,000
❀ *average number of pets owned per household:*	2.2	1.7
❀ *total number of pet animals in the US:*	81,721,000	72,114,000
❀ *average annual visits by vet to a household:*	1.7	2.6
❀ *average annual cost of vet to a household:*	$190	$356
❀ *average annual cost of vet per pet treated:*	$81	$200

——————————— THE JAGUAR ———————————

THE JAGUAR (*Panthera onca*) is the Western Hemisphere's largest cat. Heavily muscled all over, jaguars have relatively short, sturdy limbs and a deep-chested body. They are generally orange-brown with a multitude of black spots and extra black stripes on ears and tail, although completely melanistic forms are relatively common, primarily in southern areas of their distribution (in English these are known as 'black panthers'). Although jaguars are often held by outsiders to have a taste for human flesh, they are the object of reverence in many indigenous American cultures. Some tales in folklore recounts stories of men being followed for long distances through the forest by solitary jaguars – which may suggest that they are merely escorting the men off their territory rather than stalking them as prey – and further tales of jaguars coming out of the forest to play with village children. The standard diet of the jaguar would appear instead to consist mainly of deer, peccaries, birds, turtles and fish. In most countries of North, Central and South America, the jaguar is registered as an endangered and therefore protected species.

Strangely, the jaguar's name – borrowed in most other languages from Spanish and Portuguese – in the original Tupi tongue referred to any fierce carnivorous animal of a similar size, not just to the jaguar but to other large cats and even wild dogs, and the apparently akin Tupi word *aguára* refers to the crab-eating raccoon (*Procyon cancrivorus*).

——————— A CAT CAN LOOK AT A KING ———————

In old Siam, when a king died, a Siamese cat rode in the chariot at the head of the procession to crown the new king. This was because the soul of the deceased king was thought to pass into the cat, which would thus attend the coronation of the king's successor before ascending to the higher realms.

RAGDOLL CATS are a relatively modern breed of cat first produced in California, USA, in the 1960s by a cat breeder named Ann Baker who until then had concentrated on Persian cat breeds. However, a neighbour's non-pedigree longhaired cat was seriously injured in a car accident, and after her recovery consistently gave birth to kittens with highly unusual (and in human terms, desirable) personal characteristics. Ms Baker adopted three of the kittens – a male (which looked rather like a Birman) and a female of the first generation, and a female of the second generation – and from them bred what are now accepted the world over as the Ragdoll breed. The 'ragdoll' description came about because the kittens, on receiving human attention, seemed to love being stroked and became extraordinarily relaxed, even quite limp, in their enjoyment – as limp as ragdolls. For human families with children, ragdolls have been described as making ideal pets.

The three major coloration types of ragdolls are the mitted, the bicolour and the point. Some suggest their ancestry includes the Birman, but genetic research indicates the white spotting gene in ragdolls and the gene in Birmans are entirely different.

NO DOGS HERE, BY ORDER

RULE 51

Any Member introducing or causing to be introduced a dog into the Society's premises shall be liable to a fine of £5 inflicted by the Treasurer. Any animal leading a blind person shall be deemed to be a cat. Any animal entering on Police business shall be deemed to be a wombat.

Rules of the Oxford Union Society, London

SIGNS OF ILL HEALTH

There are several signs to watch for in your cat.
If any one of the following occurs, a veterinarian should be consulted:

1. *The cat eats less than usual, or stops eating altogether.*
2. *The cat avoids you, hides from you, or evidently wants to be alone.*
3. *The cat is restless, cannot settle, and does not respond in the normal way.*
4. *The cat moves and behaves quite differently from usual.*
5. *The cat has obvious physical symptoms, such as bleeding, vomiting or diarrhoea.*

HUMANS are understood to have six basic (instinctual) emotions that are linked to particular areas in the brain and/or that are responses to the sudden reactive release of hormones or other natural substances within the body. It seems the cat's emotional system is quite similar. The emotions involved are:

✯ FEAR – which enhances the outward senses and alerts the mind to the proximate dilemma of flight or fight.

✯ REPULSION – which causes cats to avoid stale or potentially toxic food (and which in humans is alternatively labelled 'disgust' and may apply to more mental subjects such as scenes or memories).

✯ LUST – which is very much concerned with hormones and pheromones.

✯ SADNESS – which in cats becomes evident as a state of depression, especially after the bereavement of a close companion or when incarcerated in unfamiliar surroundings.

✯ HAPPINESS – which in cats becomes evident as a state of contentment and, when young, as playfulness.

✯ ANGER – which in cats is not quite the same as the 'fight' reaction because, even though both may occur simultaneously, anger has a more psychological input and may last for a long time after the initial stimulus.

Some authorities suggest that in cats there is a seventh basic emotion, *frustration*, that becomes evident when for some reason any one of the six emotions above cannot be fully expressed. (Humans may after all shout, weep, stamp, or punch a wall in frustration when placed in an intolerable situation.)

———— CAT GOLD & CAT SILVER ————

CAT GOLD AND CAT SILVER are the English names of two forms of the silicon-containing group of glossy, layered minerals known collectively as mica, as translated direct from French as *or des chats* and from German as *Katzengold* and *Katzensilber*. Some of the beaches of Brittany in north-western France are naturally made up of mica sand that, under normal conditions in ordinary daylight, is grey. Yet local legend has it that sometimes in moonlight the beaches turn silver and sometimes in low sunshine the beaches turn gold – and that these colours correspond to the colours of the coats woven from the mica for the beach-fairies as punishment by twelve young men turned into cats for their presumption in joining a fairy dance on the shore.

This pleasingly folkloric background is rather spoiled by the fact that the German *Katzengold* is also a term for another group of minerals, the yellowish sulphides otherwise known in English as pyrite (fool's gold, iron sulphide), chalcopyrite (copper iron sulphide) and marcasite (brittle iron sulphide).

Ariel is frequently held to be the name of an archangel and to mean 'lion of God'. And it is certainly true that in modern Hebrew *Ari*, or *Arye*, is a name that means 'lion', and that the name Ariel is taken to mean precisely 'lion of God' (as in the name of the former Prime Minister of Israel, Ariel Sharon). But the notion that Ariel is or was the name of an archangel is contentious. It seems to have been confusion between Ariel and the genuine archangel-name Uriel that caused Ariel to be adopted into Jewish mystical lore and thence Christian and Gnostic mysticism. Much more recently it has been suggested that it is as the name of an archangel that Ariel is mentioned in the (Judaeo-Christian) Bible – a notion that has even less foundation. The sole reference to Ariel in the Bible (in Isaiah 29:1–7) is as a descriptive nickname for the city of Jerusalem, and the meaning of the first element of the name is then more likely to be 'sacrificial altar' than 'lion' anyway.

CAT NAMES IN THE UK

It has been the fashion in the UK since around 1990 for cats to be called by names that are evocatively unusual, if not downright creative. This means that few cats' names in the UK can be described as 'popular'. Nonetheless, some names have remained common, and between 2006 and 2008 they included:

FEMALE	MALE	EITHER
~~Molly~~	~~Charlie~~	~~Tigger~~
Millie	Oscar	Smudge
Willow	Tiger	Smok(e)y

What is particularly unexpected about this list is how many apparent pairs of names there are in it – Molly/Millie, Smudge/Smok(e)y, Tiger/Tigger – although the common incidence of the last two pairings might be explained by their possible reference to the coloration or markings of the cats so named.

MICROCHIP RECOGNITION

MANY CATS now have a microchip implanted in the loose skin at the shoulder so that their home details are readily available. The chip, with a capacitor and tiny aerial, is encased in a hermetically sealed tube made of biologically inert soda lime glass, no larger than a grain of uncooked rice.

When a scanner emitting radio waves is passed over the chip, the aerial detects the waves and the chip's transponder reveals its identification number on the scanner's readout. That unique number is listed against the owner's details on the regional/national cat microchip database.

SEKHMET

THE NAME OF SEKHMET, lioness (and sun and fire and war) goddess of Upper Egypt, is generally said to mean 'destructive (female)' and 'slaughtering (female)' – but the implications of her name and her divine attributes are even more sinister. For she was ordinarily described as 'the scarlet goddess' on account of her acknowledged bloodlust, and held to be patroness of menstruation in women, herself attending at the birth every morning of the blood-red rising sun. She is, probably more appropriately then, the 'bloody' goddess. No wonder she was also revered as 'the Dreaded Lady' and 'the Lady before whom Evil itself trembles'. In addition, as 'the Lady of Flame', it was her breath that heated the scorching desert winds, her arrows of fire that burned down the enemies of the pharaoh, she who was reponsible for diseases that caused fevers – and paradoxically she who was patroness of surgeons who could cauterise wounds and heal patients by sweating them. Her festivals, mostly celebrated at times when the Nile ran blood-red with silt from rains upstream, involved the drinking of vast quantities of alcohol and the subsequent drunken incapacity by her worshippers, who were obliged to make prior arrangements to be attended to by servants and others who would see them home safely. Such precautions were essential partly because these festivals took place in the temple of the lioness goddess…in areas of which real lionesses were allowed to roam.

EARLY CATS

THE EARLIEST ANCESTOR of today's cats was Proailurus ('first cat'), which looked something like a large stoat, and which, despite short legs and a long body, is reckoned to have lived in and among trees some 30 million years ago. There may have been more than one species, but the only one named is *Proailurus lemanensis*, Leman's dawn cat, fossils of which were discovered in France.

Over the next ten million years, four more genera of early cats evolved – Pseudaelurus, Sivaelurus, Pratifelis and Vishnufelis – of which only Pseudaelurus was a true ancestor of today's cats, perhaps because it seems to have been the most reproductively active genus and eventually gave rise to no fewer than ten different species of all sizes between those of a modern lynx and a modern puma.

And in due course it was also Pseudaelurus who turned out to be the forerunner not only of Schizailurus and the Felidae of today but also of the Machairodontinae – the sabre-tooth cats (*machair-odont-* 'sabre-tooth') – all of which are now extinct but which in their time were widespread across Asia, Europe, Africa and North America.

Cats are extraordinarily agile, and they make particular use of this agility when jumping. A cat can jump upwards maybe five times its own height from a crouching start. Before it does so, however, it considers exactly what is going to be necessary in carrying out the manoeuvre. Cats waste no effort (which is why they often seem merely slothful). How secure is the take-off area? Would it be better to land flat on all fours, or to get the forepaws there, dig in, and scrabble with the rear paws? Is there a better angle to reach the target from? What is the minimum power requirement for a successful leap? Are there any other contingencies to be taken into account? Not until this is all satisfactorily dealt with does the cat actually jump. Note at the same time that the cat takes it for granted that having got up to a height, it can get down again.

————————— AESTHETIC PERFECTION —————————

'Two things are aesthetically perfect in the world – the clock and the cat.'
ALAIN (ÉMILE-AUGUSTE CHARTIER, 1868–1951), *French philosopher & writer*

————————— THE CAT STANCE —————————

IN TAEKWONDO and some other martial arts, a position in which the leading foot points directly forward and the rear foot is behind it and at right-angles to it (so that the heels are closest to each other) in a sort of L-shape, the shoulders are at 45 degrees across the right-angle, and the body weight is almost entirely on the rear foot, is called the cat stance. It is a position of readiness – a transitory stance from which advance or retreat is immediately possible – it is not itself particularly stable or defensible.

————————— EAR-MAIL —————————

A cat signals its feelings by using five basic positions of the ears:

1. *Ears pointing forwards and slightly outwards* –
the cat is relaxed, but alert and listening to what is going on.
2. *Ears pricked up and pointing forwards* – the cat is alert, but ready for action
or to investigate the source of what it has heard.
3. *Ears twitching backwards and forwards* – the cat is nervous and agitated.
4. *Ears held tightly flat against the head* – the cat is irritated and defensive.
5. *Ears pricked up but slightly flattened* – the cat feels aggressive.

The five oldest cats on relatively verifiable record are:

1. **CREME PUFF**, of Austin, Texas, who is said to have celebrated her 38th birthday in August 2005.
2. **BABY**, of Duluth, Minnesota, who, according to the American Cat Fancy, celebrated her 37th birthday in 2007.
3. **PUSS**, of Clayhidon, Devon, England, who died on what was claimed to be the day after (in some versions, the day before) its 36th birthday in November 1939.
4. **GRANPA** (formally Granpa Rexs Allen), born in France but registered in Travis County, Texas, who died aged 34 years and 2 months on 1 April 1998.
5. **MA**, of Drewsteignton, Devon, England, who died aged 34 years and 1 day in 1957.

——————————— THE OCELOT ———————————

THE OCELOT (*Leopardus pardalis*) is a wild cat that is not uncommon in South, Central and southern North America, but which has also been reported in Trinidad, in the Caribbean. Because of this wide distribution it has a number of local secondary names, such as the painted leopard, McKenney's wildcat, the *jaguatirica* (in Brazil) and the *manigordo* (in Costa Rica). Hunting by night, generally along the ground but sometimes in trees, the ocelot's diet comprises mice, rats, rabbits, birds, opossums, snakes and lizards, frogs and fish, with the occasional monkey or deer. In appearance it resembles a large, long domestic cat with coat markings and coloration similar to those of the jaguar or clouded leopard. Its pelt was formerly much sought-after, which caused the ocelot to be classified as an endangered species from the 1980s to 1996 (at which time it was reclassified as of 'least concern').

The name, adopted by most other languages via French or Spanish, is originally Nahuatl (Aztec), *thalocelotl* – that is, *thalli* 'field', and *ocelotl* 'jaguar', 'tiger'.

———————— THE PROGNOSTI-CAT-OR ————————

A ninth-century Chinese proverb has it that 'If a cat washes its face and ears, it will rain.' But this is not just a folkloric method of weather forecasting, for in Chinese rural mythology what brings rain also brings good luck. The rain causes the seeds to sprout and the cereal crops to grow, with the potential result of abundant food for all.

Los Gatos is a modern town in Santa Clara County on the south-west corner of San Jose in the foothills of the Santa Cruz Mountains. Originally a small community based around a flour mill built by a Scotsman in the 1860s, the settlement was formally named Los Gatos in the 1880s, taking its name partly from the legal land-grant of 1839 that described the whole of the surrounding area as La Rinconada de Los Gatos (Cats' Junction), in apparent reference to the howling of bobcats and cougars among the nearby foothills. The population of the town was almost 28,600 in 2000, only 1 in every 19 of whom spoke Spanish. Author John Steinbeck was a resident for some years.

———————— FAMOUS CARTOON CATS ————————

The Aristocats. . . . .
Autocat. . . . .
Azrael (*The Smurfs*) . . . .
Baby Puss (*The Flintstones*) . . . .
Bagpuss . . . .
Bill the Cat . . . .
Blaze the Cat (*Bureizu za Kyatto*)
The Cat in the Hat. . . . .
The Cheshire Cat
     (*Alice in Wonderland*) . . . .
Chester Cheetah (Cheetos adverts)
Chococat . . . .
Dinah (*Alice in Wonderland*)
Eek! the Cat . . . .
The Esso tiger . . . .
Felix (cat food adverts) . . . .
Felix the Cat . . . .
Figaro. . . . .
Fritz the Cat . . . .
Garfield. . . . .
Heathcliff . . . .
Hobbes. . . . .
Isis (Catwoman's cat, as animated) .
Korky the Cat (*The Dandy*) . . . . . .
Krazy Kat . . . .
Lucifer (*Cinderella*) . . . .
Mew and Mewtwo (*Pokemon*) . . . . .

Mooch (*Mutts*). . . . .
Mr Jinks . . . .
Oil Can Harry (*Mighty Mouse*) . . . .
Peekaboo (*Rose Is Rose*) . . . .
Penelope Pussycat
     (Pepé Le Pew) . . . .
The Pink Panther . . . .
Puss in Boots (*Shrek 2*) . . . .
Rajah . . . .
Scratchy (*Itchy & Scratchy*). . . . .
Shere Khan . . . .
Si and Am. . . . .
Simba. . . . .
Snagglepuss. . . . .
Snowball (*The Simpsons*). . . . .
Stimpy (*Ren & Stimpy*). . . . .
Sylvester . . . .
Tigger. . . . .
Tom (*Tom & Jerry*). . . . .
Tony the Tiger (Kellogg's adverts) .
Top Cat (T.C.) and his gang: Benny
     the Ball, Brain, Choo-Choo,
     Fancy-Fancy, and Spook
     (*the voices of Brain and Spook
     were provided by a character
     actor named Leo De Lyon*) . . . . . .
Winston (*The Beano*) . . . .

What is frequently referred to as Rossini's 'Cat Duet' – but more authoritatively called *Duetto buffo di due gatti*, properly translated as 'Comic Duet for Two Cats' – is not a work that classical composer Gioacchino Rossini (1792–1868) would have acknowledged as his own, partly because one of its three short movements was indeed not composed by him. In fact, the two movements that are his are actually borrowed from elements – passages, not even complete movements in themselves – from his opera *Otello* (1816). The third movement is now known to be a piece called 'Katte-Cavatine' by the accomplished but little-known Danish composer Christoph E. F. Weyse (1774–1842). And the whole duet was apparently cobbled together by the equally talented but amateur English madrigalist Robert Lucas (de) Pearsall (1795–1856), who seems to have affected the byname 'G. Berthold' when doing so. The lyrics are solely repetitions of the word 'miau'.

———— THE INDOMITABLE CAT ————

'Of all God's creatures, there is only one that cannot be made slave of the leash. That one is the cat. If man could be crossed with the cat it would improve the man, but it would deteriorate the cat.'
MARK TWAIN (SAMUEL CLEMENS, 1835–1910), *US author & humorist*

———— CAT'S-FOOT PLANTS ————

Cat's-Foot is the English name (often spelled Catsfoot in the USA) of three different plants that may be translated as such in other languages.

❀ *Antennaria dioica* is a plant of the composite Asteraceae (sunflower) family with tubular white flowers sprouting from circular purple bases that might be considered reminiscent of cats' paws. Sometimes regarded as a herb, and used as a cholagogue, it is more commonly known as cat's-foot, mountain everlasting, cudweed or (regrettably) stoloniferous pussytoes. Similar species are *A. neglecta* (field pussytoes), *A. howelli* (Howell's or

Canada pussytoes) and *A. parvifolia* (Nuttall's pussytoes or Rocky Mountain cudweed).

❀ *Glechoma hederacea* is a form of creeping ivy belonging to the mint family. A native of Europe and south-western Asia, it is also common in North America where it was intro-duced as a medicinal and culinary pot herb over a century ago. Common names are ground ivy, field balm and (due to the leaf's shape) catsfoot.

❀ *Gnaphalium obtusifolium* is another member of the Asteraceae family also called cat's-foot, just catfoot, fragrant cudweed, or even rabbit tobacco.

MORE THAN HALF OF CAT OWNERS around the world never take their cat to a vet or ask the vet to visit. That is partly because cats tend to take care not to get into danger and thus avoid injury, but partly because even when they are ill, cats may hide their symptoms so that the owners are not aware of how bad they feel. This is why it is important that owners should be on the alert at all times and actively look for signs of ill health. One other consequence of this feline reluctance to admit to debility is that when cats are eventually taken to a vet, they are very often more seriously ill than other pet animals brought in (and they are therefore proportionately more likely than other pet animals to have to be put to sleep).

AESOP'S FABLE OF THE CAT & THE FOX

One day at the edge of the forest a cat and a fox were discussing their contingency plans for escaping from danger. 'I have only one plan,' said the cat, 'but it is a good plan and it is all I need.' 'You unimaginative creature!', responded the fox. 'If you were a cunning fox like me, you would have many different contingency plans, so many different ways to choose from in an emergency, and much more chance of escaping.' Just at that moment, a pack of baying hounds appeared, racing towards them. Like a streak of light the cat shot straight up the nearest tree and disappeared among the foliage. The fox, though, was so busy trying to decide which of his multiple contingency plans would be the most effective that he hardly moved before the hounds were upon him. And that was that. Up in the tree as the hounds noisily retreated again the cat shook its head, sorrowfully concluding that 'It is better to be sure of having one way to be safe than a hundred ways that might leave you sorry.'

THE RING-TAILED LEMUR

No, OK – the ring-tailed lemur is not a cat: it is a lemur. In fact, it is *the* lemur – with its black-and-white-hooped tail – the best known and most recognizable of all the lemurs of Madagascar, and taxonomically the only member of the *Lemur* genus (although all other lemurs are closely related). But it is *Lemur catta* – the specific part of its scientific name refers to it as a cat – apparently because in quite a few ways the animal behaves like a cat. Although in nature it spends some two-thirds of its time high in the trees, when walking along the ground it may hold its lengthy tail up vertically behind it (as a cat but no other mammal may do). It tends to avoid contact with water except in order to take a drink. It lives in matriarchal groups, similar to lions. And in certain circumstances it makes a noise like a domestic cat's purring.

PANGUR BÁN

THIS IS THE NAME (apparently meaning 'white trampler') of the first pet cat mentioned in European literature – albeit in pre-medieval Irish by an Irish scholar during the eighth century at or near Reichenau Abbey (on an island in Lake Constance, now southern Germany). In a poem of the same name in eight quatrains, each quatrain compares the cat's daily and nightly activities with the scholarly author's own monastic scheduled tasks.

JAGUAR GODS OF THE MAYA

The Mayas of Mexico and Central America had at least six major jaguar gods with various responsibilities and attributes, and a number of lesser jaguar deities (known as protectors and transformers). The major ones were:

✳ **God of terrestrial fire** – depicted on war shields and represented in fire rituals; personification of the number 7; possibly lord of the Underworld.

✳ **God 'L'** – an aged deity much like Graeco-Roman Pluto – associated thus both with the Underworld and with worldly wealth.

✳ **Goddess of midwifery & war**, otherwise called Ix Chel – possibly consort of the god of terrestrial fire (see above).

✳ **Patron of the month called Pax** – a deity and a month concerned specifically with war and human sacrifice; personified as a tree, he presides over the ritualized deaths of the rain deity, the principal bird diety and the vulture king.

✳ **Aged paddler** – one of two steering the canoe containing the tonsured maize (corn) god.

✳ **War hero twin deity**, otherwise known as Xbalanque – victor with his twin brother over the lords of the Underworld in a ball game.

HAUGHTY TORTIES

Most domestic cats have a coat patterning that to some degree mirrors the tabby-style markings of their wild ancestors. Over the years, however, breeders have refined these markings in respect of pedigree cats, causing them in shows to have to conform with different standards, often to increasing standards of strictness. Even in purebred tortoiseshell cats – on which the retention of some tabby markings could perhaps have been expected – the current fashion is for the black and the red coloration to be equally mixed and distributed over the body. Moreover, even more desirable in show cats these days is a patch or blaze of red or cream coloration somewhere on the face.

THE MANX CAT – of which the classic form is tailless and with a hollow or pit where, on an ordinary cat, the tail meets the body – is the result of a genetic mutation that seems to have occurred on the Isle of Man (halfway between northern England and Northern Ireland) sometime in the sixteenth century. The completely tailless Manx is often described as a Rumpy, but Manx kittens may be born with varying (if always very short) lengths of tail and may accordingly be described as Risers, Stumpies or Longies. Adult Manx cats are usually powerfully built and seem to experience no great degree of awkwardness for having no tail. However, the absence of the final vertebrae means that the whole spinal column is effectively weakened and slightly curved, and the cat has less ability to balance on narrow surfaces. Manx cats tend to bound with their hind legs together – hopping rather like rabbits – when they run, they sit back on their hind legs rather than resting on the paws, and they may suffer from chronic constipation as they reach middle age.

THE CAT-A-LOG OF INFAMY

'After scolding one's cat, one looks into its face and is seized
by the ugly suspicion that it understood every word.
And has filed it for reference.'
CHARLOTTE GRAY (1948–), *UK-born Canadian historian & writer*

CLOTHING FOR CATS

Many manufacturers who produce clothing and costumes for dogs suggest in their advertisements that their products are equally suitable for cats. It is rare to see a cat in any kind of clothing, but – taking one manufacturer's advertisement at face value – the following outfits at least are available:

✷ **Business suit**, blue or grey, with matching (floppy) hat
✷ **Chef's outfit**, with chef's cap
✷ **Rustic farmer's costume**, with (fake) straw hat
✷ **Mexican peasant costume**, with poncho–style hat
✷ **Motorcycle (fake) leathers**, with (soft fake old-style) peaked crash-helmet
✷ **Old-fashioned sailor suit**, with crocheted beret
✷ **Schoolboy shirt & shorts**, with (soft) peaked schoolcap
✷ **Swiss Alpine outfit**, with William Tell-style (fake) feathered bonnet
✷ **Tuxedo**, with (soft fake) top hat

PURRING

Cats are the only animals that purr, and do so for any of various reasons, not just to indicate contentment (see below). The sound is produced apparently by blood flow through a large vein within the chest cavity, the noise of which is amplified by air in the windpipe passing through two membranous folds (called the false vocal cords) behind the actual vocal cords. The passage of that air through the false vocal cords can be in either direction, so the cat can purr when inhaling and when exhaling and with its mouth completely closed. The larger wild cats rarely if ever purr, and if they do so they purr only for short periods: the domestic cat could purr for hours non-stop if it wanted. The average frequency of purring is 26 cycles per second (often cited as the same as that of a diesel engine when idling).

Kittens are born blind and deaf – but they can feel the vibrations of their mother's purring, and quickly learn to use it as a directional guide to finding where the milk comes from. After a week, they begin purring themselves, and the mother cat then knows that all is well. Adult cats purr mainly in anticipation of being fed or stroked, and may or may not continue when feeding or being stroked depending to an extent on whether they think it will please the people present if they go on purring.

But a cat may also purr when afraid or anxious or when in pain, although the sound may be at a very slightly lower pitch than normal. And it has been suggested by evolutionary biologists that this is an instinctual physical reaction relating to bone fractures. The frequency of the special purring in this case acts in just the same way as ultrasound can act on human bones – to promote bone growth and healing. It has long been established that cats can recover from bone injuries much faster than most other animals, contributing perhaps to the old wives' tale that cats have nine lives, and purring would now seem to be instrumental in this.

CHATOYANT

'Chatoyant' is a technical term that is used worldwide with reference to precious stones and to glossy textiles: it means 'changing colour or sheen according to the light', and is the active present participle of the French verb *chatoyer*. That verb is in turn derived from *chat-oeil*, or 'cat eye'.

THE INTERNATIONAL LION

Most of the major languages of Europe use a word for 'lion' that
conforms to one or other of the Latin variants *leo* and *leon*:

English	*lion*	Portuguese	*leão*
French	*lion*	Romanian	*leu*
Italian	*leone*		
Spanish	*león*	German	*Löwe*
		Dutch	*leeuw*
Swedish	*lejon*	Danish	*Løve*
Icelandic	*ljón*	Norwegian	*løve*
		Russian	*lev*
		Polish	*lew*
		Czech	*lev*
		Serbo-Croat	*lav*
		Bulgarian	*lev*
		Latvian	*lauva*
Finnish	*leijona*	Estonian	*lövi*
Scottish/Irish	*leon*	Welsh	*llew*
Albanian	*luan*	Basque	*lehoi*
modern Greek	*liontári*	Lithuanian	*liūtas*

NB. The word was probably initially borrowed from an ancient Semitic
language, possibly ancient Egyptian. Modern suggestions as to why the
animal was so described (e.g. 'the ripper', 'the roarer') are mere guesses.

Elsewhere, some languages have variants based
on Sanskrit *simha* ('the powerful one'):

Malay	*singa*	Swahili	*simba*
Indonesian	*singa*		
Thai	*sing*		

Perhaps compare:

Chinese	*shīzi*	Japanese	*shishi*

Whereas others are plain different:

Arabic	*asad*	Persian/Farsi	*sher*
Urdu	*asad, sheyr*	Hindi	*sher*
Turkish	*aslan*	Hungarian	*oroszlán*

In Japanese folklore, the cat is as cunning and crafty as a fox and can also change its shape to seem like another creature. This is not necessarily a bad thing – although in some cases it can be. The orange-red cat called the *kinkwa neko* or 'golden flower cat', for example, can turn itself into a woman who is beautiful to look at but who delights in eating human flesh.

SABRE-TOOTHED CATS

The sabre-toothed cat – formerly often described as the 'sabre-toothed tiger' – is any one of the three major species of the genus *Smilodon*. *Smilodon gracilis* was the earliest amd smallest of the three; *S. fatalis* was larger and was distributed more widely across the Americas; and *S. populator* was the largest of all, possibly the heaviest felid ever to have lived, and had fangs that protruded up to 17 centimetres (more than 6½ inches) from its upper jaw. They lived between 2½ million and 10,000 years ago, when the last Ice Age seems to have disrupted their normal hunting methods with the result that they became abruptly extinct. As members of the Machairodontinae subfamily, the *Smilodon* species were true cats, but they were certainly not the only sabre-toothed cats. There were several other genera, and overall two rather different types – one with long straight upper canine teeth and short, stocky limbs; the other with curving fangs and a longer, lither body and limbs. Many fossils of both types have been found, but notably of *S. fatalis* in the La Brea tar pits in Los Angeles, California.

A DEAD MOUSE FOR YOU TO ENJOY

Why do cats sometimes bring the corpses of little animals they have caught and killed and place them in a conspicuous spot indoors? Partly to show off their hunting expertise – but even more as a contribution to the household's food stocks. Adult cats in the wild bring back food to their lair for the rest of the family so that all can share in the bounty in their normal secure environment. A good reason for putting it in a visible place is that if 'the corpse' turns out not to be dead, another member of the household (ideally all standing round in admiration and gratitude) may very well catch it again. For a human, the secret is to accept 'the gift' graciously, but not so as to encourage repetition.

The practice of course represents the derivation of the cheerful English greeting between friends of 'Hullo! Look what the cat's dragged in!'

THE BIRMAN or 'sacred cat of Burma' arrived in Europe in 1919, was first recognised by pedigree authorities as a separate breed in France in 1925, but in Britain was recognized only in 1966, and by the American Cat Fancy in 1967. They are large long-haired cats with pointed colours (the classic form is the seal point, although blue, chocolate and lilac points are also extremely popular) but with pure white feet, round blue eyes, a furry tail and a light golden sheen over the coat generally. Birmans interact well with people, including children, and are by nature playfully demure and good-natured – and tolerant of other pet animals in the house.

The long-haired Birman's breed name is spelled in this way so as to distinguish it from the quite different and unconnected short-haired breed known as the Burmese.

CATS ARE FAMILY

A study of how cats and other pets are treated in the home was commissioned by a certain manufacturer of pet care products in the USA at the end of the last millennium. It found that:

* **91%** *of pet owners say they keep pets because of the unconditional love they receive from them*
* **80%** *of owners talk about their pets to other people*
* **79%** *of owners expect their pets to sleep alongside them at night*
* **68%** *of owners make decisions concerning how they spend their own lives and leisure time with reference to their pets*
* **68%** *of owners specifically regard their pets as family members*
* **47%** *of owners speak in baby talk to their pets several times per day*
* **37%** *of owners carry a photo of their pets around with them.*

GOING DOWN

A cat's claws are hook-shaped for climbing – yet it is a rare cat that realizes from the first that climbing down can be as simple as climbing up if the same procedure is used (head up and tail down) but with the limbs in reverse. Nonetheless, it is a realization that cats do tend to come to eventually, and it is extremely unusual for a cat to be genuinely stuck irrecoverably up a tree and to show enthusiasm for being rescued. (Stories of cats avoiding or resisting all the efforts of would-be rescuers, sometimes to the extent of lashing out at them, are far more common.) In the first instance, in any case, most cats prefer jumping down, although they may try to shorten the distance by reaching down with the forepaws if there is a vertical surface to push off from.

THE SENSE OF TASTE

Humans and most other mammals (including dogs) respond characteristically to any of four basic tastes: sweet, sour, bitter and salty. Cats, however, have been shown to be unable to taste sweet things – there are no sweet taste receptors in the taste nerve cellular system. A number of biologists believe that this is not so much a genetic defect as an evolutionary mutation that in some way must at some time have been hereditarily advantageous, suggesting that whatever cats might have lost by not being able to taste sweetness they surely have made up for by refining some other neural sensitivity instead (such as the sense of smell). The fact remains, though, in comparison with the sense of taste enjoyed by humans, the sense of taste in cats is poor: humans are said normally to have around 9,000 taste buds; cats apparently have only 473.

THE LEO PERSONALITY

Those mortals born under the zodiacal sign of Leo (23 July to 22 August) tend to be leaders of the pride, self-confident and commanding respect, thinking big but just as able to make the best of a bad situation not of their own making. They are fiercely loyal but expect love to be returned unquestioningly. They like attention and may even seek it, by being actors and entertainers, sometimes to the extent of seeming self-centred, headstrong and even arrogant. Leos are magnificently generous and tend to want to give lavish presents while insisting that everyone around them eats and drinks well. Generally optimistic, they may be quick to anger but are equally quick to forgive. Most love a challenge: they are natural risk-takers.

COLBY NOLAN, MBA

This six-year-old cat was awarded a Master of Business Administration degree in 2004 after a couple of researchers used his name to expose the allegedly fraudulent selling of degrees by a university in Dallas, Texas. The researchers' original application on the cat's behalf was for a bachelor's degree, costing us$299. As background, the application also stated that the cat had previously and successfully taken courses at a community college, worked at a fast-food restaurant and delivered newspapers on a paper round. The university wrote back and on the grounds of this supposed background offered the cat the Master's degree for another us$100. The cat received the degree. As one would imagine, the university was prosecuted. Its proprietors were fined, and other 'diploma mills' they owned were similarly investigated.

'There are two means of refuge from the miseries of life: music and cats.'
ALBERT SCHWEITZER (1875–1965), *German theologian, philosopher & humanitarian*

CAT BELLS, LAKE DISTRICT, ENGLAND

Cat Bells is a rounded but lump-ishly craggy mountain (a fell) in the Lake District of north-west-ern England that is popular with walkers and climbers and with sightseers viewing it from across the adjacent Derwent Water lake. From its summit, at 1,481 feet (451 metres), after a surprisingly but intermittently steep climb, a magnificent prospect extends in all directions beneath, particularly over Derwent Water to the busy tourist town of Keswick.

The 'cat' in the fell's name is a reference to the wild cats that appar-ently used to roam its slopes between the fifteenth and the nineteenth centuries, now long since gone. There never were any bells, however, for that part of the name is (probably) derived instead from Middle English *belde* (Anglo-Saxon *bieldu*), 'shelter', 'protective barrier', which indeed the fell does constitute in relation to the Newlands Valley on its eastern flank against the prevailing westerly gales.

LOUIS WAIN, CAT ARTIST & CERAMICIST

LOUIS WAIN was born in London, England, in August 1860 to a French father and an English mother. Because of a deformed ear, he received no formal schooling until the age of ten, by which time he was not interested in learning but spent most of his time wandering the streets and scrawling pencil sketches of scenes and animals on odd bits of paper. Accordingly, when he reached the age of 17 he enrolled at the West London School of Art and was successfully accredited. When his father died, Louis was obliged to become a freelance artist and illustrator to support his mother and sisters. Three years later he married one of his sisters' ex-governesses, Emily, who shortly afterwards contracted cancer and went into slow decline. To amuse Emily, he would draw her cat. And when Emily died in 1887 it was Louis' anthropomorphic cat drawings that made his reputation. The cats took on aspects of contemporary art, such as Cubist features, which lent themselves to reproduction as ceramic artworks. Louis Wain since became world famous for these strangely compelling ceramic cats. He died, in an insane asylum, in 1939.

PLANTS that are in English known as cat's-tails or cattails generally have a long, tubular flower-spike on a slender reed-like stem or have clusters of catkins – pendant inflorescences of unpetalled flowers – hanging down. The form cat's-tail is applied particularly to any of several different plants known alternatively as bulrushes, although the scientific name of the rush known as the smaller cat's-tail is *Phleum bertolonii*, and the name cat's-tails (or cat's-tail grasses) applies also to the rest of the *Phleum* genus (such as *P. arenarium* and *P. pratense*). Slightly less like bulrushes are members of the *Typha* genus, for the most part known as cattails. The graceful cattail *Typha minima* var. *gracilis*, for example, is more of a grassy reed. Plants of this genus, sometimes alternatively called reed-mack, were in parts of Europe formerly used for caulking barrels and plaiting the seats of rush-bottomed chairs. The shoots of some of them in spring are edible, apparently known in Russia as 'Cossack's asparagus'. The jelly that forms between the leaves may be used as a mild antiseptic and analgesic. There is in addition the red-hot cat's-tail *Acalypha hispida* of the spurge family, which is not like a bulrush but has long red catkins hanging down in clusters between large dark-green glossy leaves. Also unlike a bulrush is the cat's-tail aloe, *Aloe castanea*, a succulent plant which has long purple-brown flower-spikes but bright red flowers.

—— MUSICAL CATS ——

The names of the cats in the musical *Cats* by Andrew Lloyd Webber, based on T. S. Eliot's *Old Possum's Book of Practical Cats*, are:

01. Alonzo	14. Jennyanydots . . . .
02. Bombalurina	15. Macavity . . . .
03. Bustopher Jones	16. Mr Mistoffelees . . . .
04. Coricopat	17. Mungojerrie . . . .
05. Demeter	18. Munkustrap . . . .
06. Electra	19. Old Deuteronomy . . . .
07. Etcetera	20. Rumpleteazer (Rumpelteazer) .
08. Grizabella	21. Rumpus Cat . . . .
09. Griddlebone	22. (the) Rum Tum Tugger . . . . . .
10. Growltiger	23. Skimbleshanks . . . .
11. Gus (Asparagus)	24. Tantomile . . . .
12. Jellylorum	25. Tumblebrutus (Bill Bailey) . . .
13. Jemima (Sillabub)	26. Victoria . . . .

The expression 'jellicle cats', which features in the first song, is apparently based on the attempt by T. S. Eliot's infant niece to say 'dear little cats'.

LIVE CAT BOUNCE

KNOWING HOW TO LAND ON ONE'S FEET is an expression particularly associated with cats. But some cats really do take it to extremes. Some years ago, the *Journal of the American Veterinary Medical Association* reported that of a total of 132 cats that fell on average five-and-a-half storeys out of the windows or off the tops of tall buildings, 90% survived – including a cat that apparently fell 45 storeys.

HOW DID THE LEOPARD GET ITS SPOTS?

British author Rudyard Kipling (1865–1936) tells a very nice Aesop-like fable about how the leopard – as an all-over tawny-yellow-coloured animal – was obliged (after obtaining advice from a wise baboon) to take measures to assume spotty camouflage in order to be able to find, creep up on and attack formerly monochrome animals such as zebra and giraffe once those animals had taken on their camouflaging tones of blotches and stripes. Kipling concludes neatly by suggesting that the English proverbially rhetorical question 'Can a leopard change its spots?' would never have arisen if the leopard hadn't actually done it at one time in the past.

THE EYE OF THE TIGER

THE 'TIGER' was the name for the young lad who, in the early 1800s, acted as groom or rear footman when accompanying the gentleman driving the pair of horses pulling a curricle, or small, two-wheeled coach. It had a very basic rumble seat at the back in which the tiger sat, hoping not to be jolted out. The tiger was so called because he was smartly, if not garishly, dressed to attract attention when demanding immediate service (such as a fresh team of horses) on behalf of his master at coaching inns.

CATFISH are an ancient order of scaleless fish (Siluriformes) named in English – as in German *Katzenfisch*, and in French *chat marin* – after their prominent barbels that look like thick cats' whiskers... although a very few members of the order do not have such barbels. Most are freshwater fish but there are one or two marine species. Catfish have a protective sting involving a protein that in some species is highly toxic to humans. Nonetheless, catfish are an important food source all over the world, to the extent that they are farmed in the southern USA, particularly Mississippi, where the favourite recipe is breaded catfish with cornmeal, fried, and where 25 June is National Catfish Day.

THE SERVAL

THE SERVAL (*Leptailurus serval*) is a medium-sized wild cat of Africa with a startlingly small head and long legs in relation to its body size but with very tall, close-set ears. It has a spotted coat, rather than striped or banded, although melanistic individuals do occur. Its preferred habitat is savannah wherever there is also the presence of flowing water. Its diet is mostly hares, hyraxes, reptiles, birds, fish, insects and frogs, but in the wild the serval is itself often hunted by larger wild cats.

The English name 'serval' is a version of the Spanish/Portuguese *cerval*, 'like a stag', so described presumably because of the prominent ears that might look from a distance like rather rounded horns: most other European languages use variants of the same word.

ZAPAQUILDA

This enchanting female cat is the object of heartfelt desire on the part of the rival tomcats Marramaquiz and Micifuf, as described by the Spanish poet and playwright Lope de Vega (Félix Lope de Vega Carpio, 1562–1635) in *La Gatomaquia* ('The Battle of the Cats', 1634). This is a poem written in epic style – and in getting on for 3,000 verses – but actually corresponds to a parody of classical works, including Homer's *Iliad*, that recount the valorous deeds of heroes in mortal combat.

Of the two tomcats, the one presented as the outright villain of the piece is Marramaquiz, whose carnal machinations even include contingency plans to abduct Zapaquilda if necessary on her wedding night. The tomcat thus given the far more chivalrous role in Lope de Vega's poem is Micifuf, which is presumably why Micifuf remains a possible name for a cat even today among Spanish-speakers.

'One is never sure, watching two cats wash each other, whether it's affection, the taste, or a trial run for the jugular.'

HELEN THOMSON, *US cat humorist & author*

CAT ON A HOT TIN ROOF

This title of a play by Tennessee Williams (1955) refers to a state of increasingly high nervous tension in which there is a need also for extreme caution. The title is based on a nineteenth-century version ('cat on hot bricks') of a slightly earlier seventeenth-century English expression, 'cat on a hot bakestone', alluding to the hot stone or brick roofing of a pottery kiln. Cats love warmth and might well be accustomed to sit on a bakestone until it becomes too hot to endure. Such an increase in tension and discomfort is also represented in Tennessee Williams' play, in which sycophantic relatives hopeful of much-needed bequests gather for the birthday celebration of an unpleasant but dying tycoon known to them all as Big Daddy.

EXTINCT CATS

There are current difficulties with the taxonomy of cats since DNA profiling has, in recent years, caused considerable reorganization of the charting of genetic relationships within the cat family. For example, the ancestor of the subfamily Felinae – which includes the modern genus *Felis*, and thus the domestic cat – is authoritatively listed as *Felis attica* (which lived in the late Miocene, some nine million years ago in Europe and western Asia). Yet *Felis attica* is at the same time authoritatively stated to be the ancestor also of at least four other modern groups of the subfamily Felinae involving what are now the separate genera *Acinonyx* (cheetahs), *Lynx* (lynxes), *Puma* (pumas and the jaguarundi) and *Prionailurus* (leopard cats and similar). The following list of extinct cats currently classified as *Felis* species without doubt thus actually includes a majority that now ought to be reclassified in the other genera.

✱ **Felis lunensis** – Martelli's cat: a genuine wild cat, *fl.c.*12 million years ago.

✱ **Felis bituminosa** – an early puma.

✱ **Felis daggetti** – the Daggett cat: an early cougar or mountain lion – now semi-officially classified as the same as *Puma concolor*.

✱ **Felis issiodorensis** – the Issoire lynx – reclassification as *Lynx issiodorensis* has been proposed.

✱ **Felis vorohuensis** – a very early ocelot – reclassification as *Leopardus vorohuensis* has been proposed.

DO CATS REALLY EAT GRASS?

Yes, they do – and for any of a number of reasons:

✳ *It promotes emesis* – that is, it assists in vomiting up swallowed materials that are causing nausea and other purely digestive symptoms, and in coughing up furballs (hairballs) that are making breathing difficult. This is mainly because grass is almost entirely indigestible by cats who do not have the requisite enzymes to break down its high fibre.

✳ *It contains vitamins* – that is, trace amounts of vitamin A and occasionally vitamin D. Some authorities moreover claim that folic acid – one of the vitamin B complex noted for maintaining the red blood cell count – is also absorbable from grass, whereas it is not normally obtainable in a diet of meat. Cats with a tendency towards anaemia may feel better after eating grass.

✳ *It satisfies hunger* – cats may turn to grass if they are simply very hungry (or it could be the effect of an independent nutritional disorder).

✳ *They are chewing it over* – that is, they may merely be experimenting to see if the grass is nice to eat.

N B . *Cat owners should try to ensure that cats have continuous access to a patch of clean green grass outside, or even inside, the home.*

EUROCOPTER SUPER PUMA & COUGAR

EUROCOPTER is a combination of the former French company Aerospatiale and the German Deutsche Aerospace that now concentrates on making helicopters. Two of its leading products are the Super Puma and the Cougar. Intended mainly for short-hop passenger transport such as to offshore drilling rigs or conveying groups to conventions, the Super Puma AS332 is a twin-engined medium-weight civil helicopter with exceptional operational features and unusually opulent interior decor – the only modern helicopter in its class to offer a well-equipped forward lounge, a second lounge, galley and toilets, plus extra storage space. The Cougar helicopters are customized military versions of the Super Puma, capable of working as troop transports, gunships, arena surveillance platforms and anti-submarine defence aircraft.

LITTER FOR LITTERS

Kitty litter (also known as cat litter) was 'invented' by Ed Lowe in 1947 when he persuaded a neighbour in Cassopolis, Michigan, not to use sand but to try a highly absorptive clay used to soak up grease spills in factories. In 1990, Mr Lowe sold his business to Golden Cat Corporation for US$200 million.

SOCKS

You've heard the name, now see the proprietary product! Adorned with depictions of feline pulchritude, surely no cat lover of any political persuasion could fail to be moved at the thought of being clothed in such style, to ankle height anyway. Made in the USA; available via the Internet.

CAT SOUNDS

It has been estimated that an ordinary cat can make any of up to perhaps 30 different sounds, and can vary any one of those sounds according to circumstances and necessity. Cats are thus capable of a great number of vocalized expressions – there are said to be 19 different forms of 'miaow' alone, including the mewing of a kitten and the long wailing 'miaow' of a cat wanting to come in out of the rain at a closed door – which makes it all the more extraordinary that when they are by themselves; cats together rarely 'talk' (unless seriously annoyed) but rely mainly on body language and scent. The number and type of sounds that any individual cat makes therefore generally depends on what it has learned to do in the company of humans. Recognizing that humans rely on sound communication, cats quickly learn which noises elicit desirable responses from humans and go on to build up a vocabulary accordingly, naturally based mainly on the 'miaow' that is the first sound they make as kittens with their mother. When a cat miaows to make its needs or intentions plain to a human, it is, in effect, talking baby-talk so the human will understand.

LET THE CAT OUT OF THE BAG

TO LET THE CAT OUT OF THE BAG is an eighteenth-century English expression that means 'to accidentally or unwittingly reveal a secret'. Remarkably, it has an exact counterpart in German – *die Katze aus dem Sack lassen* – although there is no such correspondence in French or most other languages. Perhaps that is because in former centuries the Germans, like the English, were crafty market traders. For the expression is derived from the practice of selling piglets in a poke basket or sack at the local market. A purchaser would have to take on trust the vendor's word that there was indeed a piglet – and not a worthless cat – inside the sack ('a pig in the poke'). But if the vendor had actually substituted a cat for the little piggy that went to market, and the purchaser then insisted on seeing the animal before completing the purchase – or if the animal itself somehow managed to get out of the sack and escape – either way, the cat would truly be let out of the bag, and the truth would become apparent.

The *Panthera* genus evolved around three million years ago, and those that have survived have since become today's big cats. But quite a few have not survived, including the several large species now generally called cave lions. Possibly the most significant is thought to be *Panthera leo fossilis*, which roamed across Asia, Europe and northern Africa some 500,000 years ago and which may or may not have further evolved into the big cat classified as *Panthera leo youngi* (rarely described in full as the North-Eastern Pleistocene China cave lion). This cat flourished 350,000 years ago and may be genetically connected with both the European cave lion (*P. l. spelaea*, the true cave lion) and the American cave lion (*P. l. atrox*), both of which lived around 300,000 years ago. Cave lions as such generally became extinct during the last Ice Age 10,000 years ago – at the beginning of which the lion was the world's most widespread large land mammal (besides humans) – but it is likely their genes remain extant in several of the eight sub-species of lions recognized by most authorities today.

HAIR-RAISING EXPERIENCES

WHEN A CAT IS VERY FRIGHTENED, its hair may stand up stiff over its entire body, right down to the paws. When a cat resolves to attack another cat (or a dog), its hair may stand up stiff in a line along the ridge of its back and the top of its tail. Biologists think that this second situation represents an extreme form of the body language cats use in relation to each other – an instinctive way for the cat to make itself look taller and thus more menacing. The effect is caused by the contraction of tiny muscles under each hair.

NGARIMAN

According to the legends of the Karadjeri people of Australia, one of the creatures encountered by the Bagadjimbiri brothers – who in the Dreamtime were travelling the world even as they created it – was Ngariman, the cat-being. Ngariman looked so strange to the brothers that they burst out laughing. (Perhaps it should be remembered that the cat-being would have been akin to the quoll, or marsupial 'tiger cat'.) They laughed so raucously that Ngariman was mortally offended. He called up his cat-being relatives and together they killed the Bagadjimbiri brothers. The earth goddess Dilga observed this, and was moved to intervene. From her breasts flowed a torrent of milk that drowned all the cat-beings and resuscitated the fortunate Bagadjimbiri brothers.

Cᴀᴛ'ꜱ ᴄʀᴀᴅʟᴇ is the common English name for a game in which a framework of cords or strings is stretched across the fingers of both hands and altered symmetrically by rearrangement in set figures (also known in some parts of the USA as Jack-in-the-pulpit). It is from one such set figure, often alternatively called 'diamonds', that the name of the game is derived. Similar if not identical games – almost always involving the additional transfer of the string framework from the hands of one person to the hands of another – are known all over the world.

Probably because of its similarly diamond-based form, the show-riding (gymkhana) course for horses and ponies known as a cat's cradle requires riders to negotiate a figure-of-eight path around the points of a diamond figure marked out on the ground.

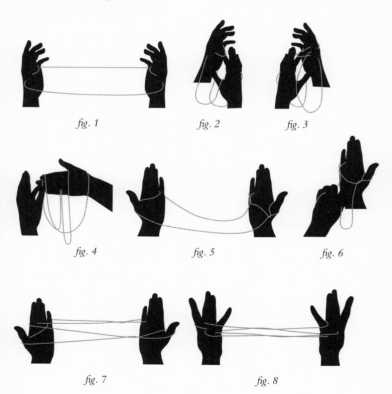

fig. 1   fig. 2   fig. 3

fig. 4   fig. 5   fig. 6

fig. 7   fig. 8

CAT-SCRATCH FEVER

THIS FORTUNATELY RARE bacterial infection is contracted by humans after being scratched by a cat. The symptoms – which generally appear at least a week after the scratch was made – include a high temperature with chills, swelling of the lymph nodes (those parts of the body's immune system that attempt to contain and dispose of the invading bacteria), and an overall feeling of being unwell ('hot and bothered') that may persist for up to a fortnight after the other symptoms have cleared up. Medical treatment is usually only to reduce the high temperature. For many years the disorder was thought to be caused by a virus, being defined as a bacterial infection only in the 1950s. The causative bacterium (the alpha-proteobacterium *Bartonella henselae*) was itself only identified in the last 15 years of the twentieth century.

ANCIENT EGYPTIAN CAT NAMES

THE ANCIENT EGYPTIANS were the first people to invite cats into their homes and feed them on a regular basis – provided that they earned their keep and got rid of any snakes, lizards, mice and other unwelcome creatures that might find their way onto the premises. It is only right, then, that the earliest name known for a cat comes from within that culture. Unfortunately, the name most commonly cited as the earliest cat name – Bouhaki, apparently from *bou*, 'house' and *hak*, 'divine ruler', and said to date from around 2000 BC – has recently been determined instead to be the name of a dog. Nonetheless, the name Nedjem (meaning 'star' according to some commentators, and 'sweet' or 'pleasing' according to others) *was* given to a cat who lived in the reign of the pharaoh Thutmose III, 1479–1425 BC.

ERNEST HEMINGWAY ON CATS

'One cat just leads to another.'
ERNEST HEMINGWAY (1899–1961), *US author & journalist*

Cats have evolved to be active hunters devoted to the frenetic chasing and catching of prey. The energy they spend in doing this takes a heavy toll: it shortens their lifespan by a considerable margin. That is why even a domestic cat that spends its life outdoors as a semi-feral or feral may live no longer than an average of three years, whereas an indoor cat that has no worries at all about where the next meal is coming from generally lives *at least* five times longer. A lion in the wild tends to have a lifespan of between 10 and 14 years, but a lion in a comfortable zoo may well reach the age of 25 or 26 before succumbing. The lifespan of the less sociable tiger in the wild is only eight to ten years, but in the benign surroundings of a zoo may likewise extend to 25 or 26.

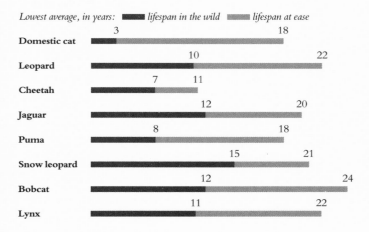

Lowest average, in years: ■ *lifespan in the wild* ■ *lifespan at ease*

Domestic cat	3	18
Leopard	10	22
Cheetah	7	11
Jaguar	12	20
Puma	8	18
Snow leopard	15	21
Bobcat	12	24
Lynx	11	22

—— ANNE FRANK & HER CATS ——

When, in July 1942, Anne Frank's family moved into a 'rear annexe' secret hideout in Amsterdam to escape being arrested and transported by the occupying Germans as Jewish stateless nationals, they were joined by a number of other ex-German emigrants – and two cats, which they named Boche and Tommy. These names are surprising because they represent the slang words used by Britons and Germans respectively for each other's footsoldiers in the trenches during World War I, and neither is Dutch. The fugitives were joined also by a third cat, which was called Mouschi – an even more unusual name, again not Dutch, that looks as if it ought to be pronounced in a French manner.

THE CATSKILL MOUNTAINS

THE CATSKILL MOUNTAINS form the eastward continuation, and the highest element, of the Allegheny Plateau in New York State, USA, a short drive north-west of New York city. In the east they rise steeply from the Hudson Valley, and it is in this area that there are more than 30 peaks above 3,500 feet (1,067 metres), the highest – Slide Mountain, in Ulster County – at 4,180 feet (1,274 metres). It is taken for granted by virtually all American geographical commentators that the 'Cat' in Catskill does indeed refer to some sort of cat, probably a bobcat but possibly a mountain lion, and that the name is derived from *Kaatskil*, a name given to the area by the seventeenth-century Dutch settlers and universally held to mean 'cats creek' in Dutch. However, there are some fairly weighty objections to this, not least that *Kaatskil* could never have meant 'cats creek' in Dutch, that the Dutch settlers meant the name to apply to the glens and dells of the area and not to a waterway or the mountains at all, and that bobcats and mountain lions have always been conspicuous by their absence in the area.

'WE ARE SIAMESE, IF YOU PLE-EASE'

'The Siamese Cat Song' was a popular song in the late 1950s that featured in the Disney animated film *Lady and the Tramp*. The film's screen format was the widest ever used in any Disney production, which emphasized the finely delineated thinness and height of the two disdainful Siamese cats that sang the song. Both cats' voices were supplied by the song's co-writer, actress-singer Peggy Lee, who, with Sonny Burke, provided all the film's lyrics and music. It has been suggested that it may be the most popular cat song ever recorded.

MOROCCAN PROVERB

In Morocco, the equivalent of 'You can't teach an old dog new tricks' is 'An old cat will not learn how to dance'.

CHEETAHS IN TITIAN'S ART

The ancient Greek god Dionysus is often described in Greek texts as accompanied by tigers, panthers or leopards or, less commonly, lynxes, because he is the deity who represents the connection between the human and the animal worlds. The god of the totally animalian is Pan, the god of the ideally intellectual human is Apollo, and between them is Dionysus, the god of those humans who leave their humanity behind and *become* animals (or at least less than the free-willed humans they were) through passion, drink, madness or role-play – for Dionysus was also god of the theatre. However, although cheetahs were known in ancient Greek times, they were never cited as attendant on Dionysus (or Bacchus, as he was also known) and the question therefore arises: why does the much later Renaissance painter Titian include two of them in his celebrated painting *Bacchus and Ariadne* (1520–1523)? And why are they the most calm – not to say detachedly disinterested – elements in a painting otherwise characterized by frenetic activity? The probable answer is mundane: because his patron for the painting had just received two such animals as pets, and when used as models they were still cowed by their unfamiliar surroundings.

THE GEMSTONE known to jewellers as the cat's eye is the chrysoberyl, which, when rounded and polished, is a brightly reflecting golden yellow colour that appears to shimmer or change shade towards or away from a greenish tint according to the angle it is seen from, altogether remarkably similar to the eyes of some cats. 'Chrysoberyl' is derived from Greek words meaning 'golden beryl', yet the mineral is not actually a silica-based beryl (like emerald or aquamarine) but an admixture of aluminium oxide with beryllium, which is also superior in hardness (8.5 on the Mohs scale).

To mineralogists, the mineral known as the cat's eye – or the tiger's eye – is either of two varieties of crocidolite, a composite mineral that occurs as the result of compression and oxidation within a crack between harder, different materials (such as quartz), and is basically made up of sodium, iron and magnesium that have been partly silicified. It is found only in South Africa, where it is also called fibrous Riebeckite asbestos.

———————— THE REAL CAT'S EYE ————————

CATS have the largest eyes of all mammals in relation to the size of their skull – but they have no eyelashes. Humans have eyelashes to protect the eyes from airborne objects or liquids, and when the eyelids are shut, the eyelashes above and below the eyes thus meet together. Cats don't normally close their eyes by bringing down the eyelids, however. Instead they do the equivalent of bringing their eyebrows right down over the eyes, and the fur above and below the eyes, meeting together, acts as far better protection than eyelashes would. Nonetheless, cats do have eyelids – for each eye an outer one that is the equivalent of the human eyelid, and an inner one (the nictitating membrane, for some reason also known as 'the third eyelid') that is generally only visible in part when the cat is very sleepy or feeling particularly unwell.

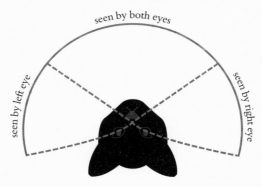

'Play with a cat – and ignore the scratch.'
Yiddish proverb

AESOP'S FABLE OF THE LION & THE MOUSE

A LION was abruptly awakened from his sleep when a mouse ran over his face. He rose up, caught the rodent and was about to despatch the creature when the mouse spoke up. 'Please, sir, spare my life and I will in turn perform a service that will repay you for your kindness.' The lion, astonished but also amused, let the mouse go. Not long after this episode the lion was entrapped by hunters, who pegged him with ropes to the ground. It also so happened that the mouse was within hearing distance of the lion's roar, recognized it, and came swiftly forward to gnaw through the ropes and thus set the lion free, exclaiming as it did so, 'You really didn't think I could make good my promise to do you an important service, but now I have done – a mouse can indeed be a Good Samaritan to a lion.' The lion had to admit to himself that no creature is so insignificant as to be unable to offer significant help to another.

THE SEAFARING CAT

It is thought that Phoenician cargo ships first transported the domestic cat from North Africa (and probably from ancient Egypt, where the Phoenicians were inveterate traders) to Europe sometime in the early first millennium BC.

It would seem to be the case that the Pilgrim Fathers were the first to introduce domestic cats to North America on their arrival in New England in 1620, although the Native Indians they encountered there were already well aware of the existence of wild cats, using their skins as clothing. The Pilgrims' cats were presumably brought from England, although the first port of embarkation for the majority of Pilgrims going to America was in Holland.

THE RESPONSIVE CAT

It is said that cats remember better and respond more readily to their names if their names end in the vowel sound 'ee', and if spoken by a woman rather than a man. Whereas the first part of that suggestion is likely to be quite untrue (and would depend on the home language anyway), the second part may correspond to a cat's natural preference for the higher pitch of voice.

MORE A BEAR THAN A CAT – but not actually either – the animal sometimes called the cat bear (or, indeed, the bear-cat) is in fact the lesser or red panda, additionally known as the fire-fox, an endangered species that lives in the mountains of central, southern and eastern Asia and which resembles an outsize raccoon.

Its scientific name has distinctly feline connections: *Ailurus fulgens*, literally 'lightning-flash cat'. Like its relative, the giant panda, it relies on bamboo for its food and its population has been declining as bamboo-growing areas are reduced by human encroachment and through illegal hunting. Amazingly, it was the cat bear that was first given the name 'panda', in 1821, albeit as a corruption of a dialectal Chinese name for it, *pun-ya*.

CAT FLU

FOR DECADES, this flu has been acknowledged as a major disorder for cats. One problem with the description is that flu in humans may be comparatively far less serious. In general, cat flu is caused by either of two viruses (the herpes virus or the rhinotracheitis virus, although there are alternatives). Cats affected may suffer from running noses or eyes, fever and malaise, coughing and sneezing, and disinterest in eating. There may also be ulceration of the tongue, nose and hard palate, and running of the eyes. It may turn out to be especially virulent in cats who have long-standing gum disease. However, since the 1980s there have been several bacterial infections that have been reported to give rise to identical symptoms (including for instance infection by *Bordetella bronchoseptica*), and secondary bacterial infections are in any case not uncommon following the viral infection, although these at least are responsive to veterinary drug treatment. Household therapy for a cat with cat flu is above all to encourage the cat to eat and drink as normally as possible. If breathing becomes difficult for the cat, try steam treatment (by which the cat inhales steam to help break up mucus in eyes and nose) – but avoid oils.

Vaccination is generally the best prevention of cat flu, but it has to be on an annual basis. Even if it does not prevent an outbreak of cat flu, it should ensure that those cats who suffer from the disorder do so less harmfully. Symptomless sufferers of cat flu may nonetheless pass on the disease if they undergo times of particular stress, such as when moving home or being boarded at a cattery.

IN MEMORIAM

In an ancient Egyptian household, when the family cat died, all members of the family would shave their eyebrows as a sign of mourning.

BY THE SCRUFF OF THE NECK

MOTHER CATS carry straying kittens back to the 'nest' by using their jaws to grasp the fold of loose skin at the back of the neck, and lifting them up bodily by it. Because it is loose skin, and because the kittens' overall weight is slight, no harm is done, no pain is felt, and the mother licks each kitten on releasing it to ensure that no emotional damage is done either. All kittens thus in time are conditioned to become 'instinctively' submissive when grasped by the scruff of the neck and remain so from then on. There are two things humans should remember about this when taking it upon themselves to lift an adult cat by the scruff of the neck for any reason. Adult cats are much heavier than kittens, and not only will the pressure of the grasp at the neck have to be far more forceful to lift the cat, but the cat will feel it as a painful squeeze that may induce choking. And even if the lift by the human is not after all particularly painful, it represents a form of maternal domination of the cat that requires maternal pacification afterwards – a cuddle or a stroke at the very least – *especially* if the cat was grabbed at a scene of combat with another cat.

THE AMERICAN HOUSECAT

It was in 1987 that cats finally outnumbered dogs in American homes and so became the number-one pet there. Twenty-one years later, cats were recorded as outnumbering dogs by more than ten million, and around 40% of all American homes had at least one cat.

THE CARACAL

A medium-sized wild cat often known inaccurately as the Persian or African lynx, the caracal is not actually related to lynxes but is like them in having dark tufts on its ears. In fact, this is how it got its name, from the Turkish *karakulak*, 'black ears' – hence the scientific name *Caracal caracal*. Described as medium-sized, the wily caracal is in fact comparatively small but heavy, remarkably fast-moving and agile. Its closest relative is the serval. The caracal lives mainly in Africa and western Asia, in fairly dry surroundings. Amazingly, this cat requires no fluids other than those ingested from prey, which are mostly hyraxes, rodents and birds, although it may go for the occasional deer or ostrich.

The first long-haired breed to have emerged naturally in the USA, the Maine Coon is a large, tough, hardy cat with a rugged coat and very furry tail. It is likely that the ancestors of the Maine Coon arrived in North America from Europe (or possibly western Asia) during the eighteenth century. Classic colorations are brown tabby or silver tabby, but other colorations are now common. The first Maine Coons to be put on show outside the USA were exhibited in what was then West Germany in 1978, and when they were first exhibited in Britain, in 1984, they were described as American Forest Cats. Nonetheless, more than 60 different colour and patterning combinations have so far been ascribed to the Maine Coon.

DO CATS DREAM?

WHEN THEY SLEEP, cats go through phases of dreaming in just same way as humans do, during periods of deeper sleep. It is not possible – because of the way cats close their eyes to sleep – to detect the rapid eye movements behind the eyelids, but other giveaway signs may manifest as twitching paws, claws and whiskers, a flick of the ears, or even a slight moan.

CATS FEELING THE COLD

Although there are sensor cells that detect heat and cold all over a cat's body, its thick covering of fur means that a cat is relatively insensitive to what humans think of as extremes of heat and cold – except on its face (its nose and eyes) and its forepaws. To avoid a lower temperature in disparate parts when going to sleep a cat may bring round its tail to cover its nose and rest its chin on its forepaws so that these sensitive areas maintain an equable warmth. A cat that likes to snuggle down in a human lap may also find it unacceptable if the lap is unexpectedly too cold for its forepaws. Similarly, cat food should always be served at or above room temperature – food and drink straight from the fridge may be ignored completely until it has warmed up.

HOT CATS

Cats have no sweat glands in the skin, only in the pads of their paws. To cool down, cats can only pant and lick their fur, letting the saliva evaporate.

TUCKER SNO-CATS comprise a family of hardy, fully enclosed four-tracked vehicles for use as personnel transport and in towing sledges across rough snow-covered terrain. Mostly powered by 170-horse-power diesel engines using automatic transmission to drive the four tracks which are slung in pairs fore and aft on two rotatable axles within 'pontoons', with each pontoon independently able to articulate over very uneven surfaces, Sno-Cats can carry up to eight people and tow weights of up to eight tonnes. They are extremely useful in Arctic and Antarctic regions, but are also to be found in many ski resorts and mountain nature parks, although in the latter locations substitutes made by competitors, some with only two tracks, and known under the general name of snowcats, may be equally common.

CAT-NAV

DO CATS HAVE A SIXTH SENSE? Dogs are sometimes said to be able to tell when 'the master' on his way home from work is within a mile of the house, and they go to wait at front door or window to greet him – but are cats capable of anything like that? Actually, there *are* stories of cats that do precisely the same thing. But one subtle sense that cats have, and dogs don't, is an inborn ability to find their way back from unknown territory to a familiar location. There are literally hundreds of factually evidenced anecdotes of cats who for one reason or another have been accidentally left behind in some remote and alien landscape, and who have somehow made their way back – sometimes over astonishing distances – to be reunited with their human family. It has been suggested that cats have the same sort of magnetic directional orientation as homing pigeons (although pigeons also rely on the sun), which implies a constant knowledge of exactly where they are on the global map, plus a highly accurate memory for the precise positions of other known locations.

But even this would not explain the recorded and evidenced ability of far fewer cats who have taken it upon themselves to travel from familiar ground to completely foreign territory in order to successfully find loved humans who had moved away and left them behind. They can do it – but how they do it remains a mystery that may never be explained.

BEWARE OF THE CAT

While a cat bite is less common than a dog bite, a cat bite on a human is statistically more likely to become infected than a dog bite, partly because whereas dogs clean their teeth by chewing, cats cannot chew – they can only bite with an up-and-down motion of the lower jaw.

Almost all major languages of the world reckon that a cat emits a 'miaow', even if the spelling differs slightly according to the speakers' own linguistic tradition and sense of phonetic correctness – as, for example:

German	.miau	**Dutch**	miauw
French	miaou	**Afrikaans**	miaau
Swedish	.mjau	**Italian**	miao
Icelandic	mjá	**English alternative**	meow
Croatian	mijau	**Catalan**	meu
Turkish	miyauw	**Vietnamese**	meo

This is a list of *different* spellings: many other languages
spell the word in one of these ways.

But of the comparatively few major languages that do not follow the general rule, it is remarkable how many nevertheless make use of a variant of the same onomatopoeic word that begins instead with n-:

Modern Greek	niaou	**Hungarian**	nyávogás
Tagalog	nyaw	**Arabic**	nau
Japanese	nyaa, nyan	**Estonian**	näu
Indonesian	ngeong		

– while Czech- and Slovakian-speakers try to have it both ways: *mňau*

—————— EDWARD LEAR'S PUSSYCAT ——————

Edward Lear (1812–88), born in London as the twentieth child of his poor but middle-class parents, was primarily an illustrator and artist, yet became a celebrated writer of 'nonsense' verse. His most famous poem, *The Owl and the Pussycat*, was written in 1867 for the children of his patron, the Earl of Derby, and has since been translated into many languages. (The website http://bompa.org quotes over 70 different versions in more than 60 languages.) What is less well known, however, is that some of his inspiration for the poem – and for many little sketches and one or two limericks – came from his own pet cat, a striped tabby he called Foss (apparently as an abbreviation of the Greek *adelphos*, 'brother'). So fond of Foss was Mr Lear that when, in 1870, he moved for the sake of his health – he was a lifelong epileptic – to San Remo, Italy, he instructed an architect to design his new residence to be identical to the one he was leaving behind in England. This way, Foss would find the move as minimally stressful as possible. When Foss died – only ten weeks or so before Mr Lear did – he was buried in the garden of the Italian house.

In southern Peru, the Quechua-speaking Indians tell of a terrible cat-like demon called Ccoa who lives in the highest parts of the mountains and from there sends down rain, hail and thunderbolts to ravage the crops in the cereal fields of the valleys far below and cause the local inhabitants to go hungry and cold. Worse still, in northern Ecuador the Indians there believe that Ccoa sometimes descends to the valleys in person where he rapes and strangles any woman unlucky enough to be caught out on her own. Despite this fearsome reputation, however, Ccoa is described as only about a metre (just over three feet) long, but he has a large head and stripes that run the length of his body. Fortunately, he can be appeased (or at least distracted) by regular votive offerings left out for him at the bottom of the mountain slopes.

———————— SPAYING & NEUTERING ————————

The trouble these days about *not* spaying or neutering your non-pedigree cat is that you are then responsible for dealing with the unwanted progeny that duly and regularly arrive thereafter. It is neither politically correct nor, in many countries, legal for a non-veterinarian simply to kill kittens as soon as they are born. Moreover, apart from the obvious effect, there are additional advantages in spaying and neutering, and (despite some folklore) very few disadvantages.

It is pure myth that a spayed/neutered cat will become fat and lazy – if so, it is almost always because the owner has cossetted it. It is also untrue that females, on grounds of physical health, should be allowed to have one litter. Statistics prove that females spayed before their first heat turn out to be healthier through life. It is not true, either, that a male cat when neutered will feel any less male. Cats do not have that kind of emotional concept of sexual identity. In the same way, a spayed female will never miss having (more) kittens.

Outright advantages of neutering a male cat include:

※ *The cat is far less likely to fight with other males*
※ *The cat is far less likely to spray strong urine*
※ *The cat will never suffer from some serious feline diseases and disorders,
including some relatively common forms of cancer*
※ *The cat is likely to have a longer, healthier life altogether*
※ *The cat is less allergenic in respect of susceptible humans*

Outright advantages of spaying a female cat include:

※ *The cat will never suffer from some serious feline diseases and disorders,
including some relatively common forms of cancer*
※ *The cat is likely to have a longer, healthier life altogether*

Why does a cat roll over and invite you to stroke its stomach? It is a gesture of trust, and only happens when a cat is thoroughly confident of your affection and wishes to reciprocate. It is effectively a supreme compliment to you, and may have additional connotations of a warm greeting or an invitation to play.

———————— TRAINING A CAT ————————

DESPITE THE FACT that cats are determined individualists and take no pleasure in being 'obedient' (as dogs may), it is quite possible to train a cat to recognize its name and to come on command. Less usefully, it is certainly also possible to train a cat to perform a number of different tricks and procedures. The earlier in the cat's life you start the training, the greater the chances are of success, but you should remember throughout that training is something of a joint activity – both you and the cat are finding out how to make each other respond in a way that works for you together – and that to some extent the cat is therefore simultaneously training you, too.

The primary method of training is to use rewards, generally in the form of favourite foods or food treats. The cat should be rewarded every time it carries out a new task successfully. Once the procedure has been learned, the reward should be forthcoming less often, perhaps only when performance is specially good or at the end of a training session. Training sessions should not be long – around 15 minutes is said to be ideal – but should, if possible, take place once a day, and should follow an identical pattern on each occasion. Longer than 15 minutes and the cat (and/or you) may become bored. Sessions should also be before or well away from any set mealtimes so that the cat has some appetite for its rewards. Remember that the training is to get the cat to respond to your vocal commands – and make sure that those vocal commands are properly audible by turning off any radio, TV or other audio equipment within range.

Finally, remember also that training a cat requires love, consistency, patience, authority, repetition and of course reward – but never punishment.

———————— THE CARPAL PAD ————————

THE CARPAL PAD is the area of pad tissue a third of the way up the back of a cat's leg ('on the palmar surface of each carpus') that may be used for additional traction when coming to an abrupt halt in mid-run or when cautiously slithering forwards down a steep slope.

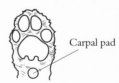

Carpal pad

The underside of a lion's paw

THE HONOURABLE CAT MANDU

It is likely that the ginger tabby Cat Mandu is the only cat ever to have been formally elected to political office. Until his untimely death in a road accident in 2002, he belonged to Alan 'Howling Laud' Hope with whom he was, in a ballot of all party members, jointly elected leader of the Official Monster Raving Loony Party in the UK after the demise in 1999 of the party's charismatic founder, Screaming Lord Sutch. Mr Hope has since soldiered on alone in the post, very creditably, according to some – and it can only be conjectured whether Cat Mandu would have made an even greater mark on British politics if it had been Mr Hope who had suffered the fatal accident and not the unfortunate ginger tabby.

THE CAT'S EYE NEBULA

THE CAT'S EYE NEBULA (NGC 6543) is a classic but complex planetary nebula visible (via the Hubble telescope) in the constellation Draco as a diaphanously luminescent circular entity more than half a light-year across, an X-ray source at its centre representing the final phase of a star that would once have been like our own sun, some 3,000 light-years away.

THE CLOUDED LEOPARD

For a relatively small wildcat, the clouded leopard is comparatively well-built yet extremely agile. It lives mainly among the tropical mountain forests of the Himalayas, China, and south-east Asia, down to Borneo – although the Bornean clouded leopard is a different species (*Neofelis diardi*) from the mainland clouded leopard (*Neofelis nebulosa*), the only two members of the *Neofelis* genus. The diet normally comprises small deer, monkeys, wild pigs, fish, squirrels and porcupines, but it will take domestic cattle and chickens if it gets the chance. It is the only cat known to be able to climb down trees head first, and to use its tail not merely as a counterbalance when walking along thin branches but as some measure of lateral support. In proportion to its skull and skeleton size, the clouded leopard has the longest canine teeth of all living cats – to such a degree that it has been suggested that, given a couple of million more years of evolution, it might turn into the next sabre-tooth. Unhappily, it is already on the 'vulnerable' list of endangered species.

It is called the clouded leopard because of the strange net-like markings on its back and sides, quite unlike the markings of any other kind of cat and, close up, nothing like clouds either – but apparently sufficiently cloud-like from a distance, and especially from beneath, for the name, once given, to have stuck. However, genetic research has revealed that it is not even a particularly close relative of the leopard.

There are no fewer than three alternative derivations for the name of the rock-strewn channel between northern Denmark and southern Sweden – and two out of three concern cats.

It is apparently a Danish tradition that the name is derived from what Dutch sailors first called the channel: the equivalent of 'cat gut', a narrow and winding passage through which it was difficult to navigate, and (presumably) with rocks and islets spiky enough also to be reminiscent of the claws of a cat.

On the other hand, the Swedes and Norwegians are said to believe that the name comes directly from Old Norse *kati*, or 'boat' and *gata*, or 'street', 'path', 'course' – it was the only way through for boats travelling between the Baltic Sea and the Skagerrak and the North Sea. The connection with cats here is strictly etymological, for the Old Norse *kati* is ultimately derived from the early medieval Latin *catta*, a small boat (probably) so called because from immediately in front the wide, rounded bows had a cross-sectional shape much like a cat's head. (It is this connection between a cat's head and the bows of a boat that has historically given rise to such nautical expressions as 'catwalk', 'cathead', 'catblock' and 'catfall'.)

The third potential derivation is historically the first, for it relates to what the Kattegat was named on ancient Roman maps: *Codanus Sinus*, or 'the Bay (or channel) of Coda(n)'. Some authorities think that 'Codan-' might be an early corrupt form of 'Scandin-' (as in Scandinavia, earlier *Skaden-awje*), but no one knows for sure – and even if Coda(n) does correspond to Katte-, it still leaves the second element open to other interpretations.

THE CARTOON STRIP GARFIELD was created in 1978 by the US cartoonist Jim Davis, who apparently named the cat partly after his own grandfather, James Garfield Davis. Within three years, *Garfield at Large* – the first Garfield book – was listed in the *New York Times* bestseller list at number 1, and within a further three years the Garfield strip was syndicated to more than 1,400 newspapers. By 2002 the Garfield strip was deemed worthy of inclusion in the *Guinness Book of Records* for its worldwide ubiquity, mostly featuring the cat under his American name (although in Norway he is known as Pusur, in Sweden as Katten Gustaf and in Finland as Karvinen). Some of this popularity may well stem from the feline's all-too human traits of laziness, self-absorption and an unhealthy love of lasagna.

'Tiger Rag' is the name of a jazz standard (tune) first recorded in 1917 by the Original Dixieland Jass [sic] Band but made internationally popular through a second recording in 1918 by the same outfit, by then called the Original Dixieland Jazz Band. Even at the time of the first recording, however, the number was well known to jazz bands around the USA, particularly in New Orleans. By the 1920s, hundreds of different recordings of 'Tiger Rag' were commercially available, including arrangements for dance bands and as a military march. During the 1930s the tune was taken up by Big Band arrangers, lyrics were added, and as a song 'Tiger Rag' was performed by some world-famous artistes, such as Louis Armstrong. By 1942, the number was an acknowledged standard with more than 135 different cover versions on record. It lost popularity during the Swing era, having become something of a cliché, but revived a little during the late 1950s and early 1960s, and today remains a popular theme tune for professional sports teams that have the word 'Tigers' in their name.

WHERE DO SOME CATS HAVE MORE LIVES?

In English-speaking parts of the world it is an acknowledged fact that a cat has nine lives. But in countries where the language is Latin-based (particularly in Italy and Spain) cats by long-standing tradition have only seven.

NO SUBORDINATE CLAWS

CATS are the only animals that walk on claws, although the pads of the paws also come in contact with the ground (causing pawprints). Other animals that walk on the equivalent of human finger- and toe-nails have hooves, not claws. But that is why it is essentially mistaken to describe cats as 'digitigrade' (as they generally are described) when they are *not* actually walking on the fingers or toes. Walking on their claws, however, means that they are always ready for action, ready to spring, ready to pounce. And the claws have to be kept sharp. Yet that is not why cats use a scratching post – or the garden fence or the leg of your favourite chair or table. No: just as human nails may be kept sharp and in good condition not just by cutting them across the top appropriately but also by cleaning out the odd bits of skin growth at the edges and base, so cats when they scratch tree-trunks or antique umbrella-stands are removing the ragged edges of the sheaths of their claws. Every now and then, though, an old claw detaches ('sheds') altogether to expose a shiny new claw beneath it. (Make sure that the children of your household are aware that it is *not* the same as a human nail coming off whole.)

HOUSECATS, unable to use body language or scent as they do perfectly well with other cats, learn to create for themselves a vocabulary of sounds to alert humans to what they want or what they mean to do. It is a slow, two-way process, as through trial and error a cat learns what works and what doesn't, and a human finally makes sense of at least some of the messages being sent. Yet cats have different personalities and this, too, affects how much they will communicate with humans. Some cats may decide that communication, apart from in emergencies, is just not worth the bother; others may reckon that they get most of what they want anyway, and there is simply no need to make a further effort.

BEAUTY & THE BEAST

Aesop tells how a lion fell in love with a beautiful maiden and, deciding to do the thing properly, visited her parents to ask for her hand in marriage. The folk were much taken aback. They didn't want to give their daughter to the lion, yet they did not want to offend the King of Beasts. At length, the girl's father spoke up: 'Sir – I mean, Your Majesty – we are highly sensitive of the honour you are doing us by making this proposal, and in principle we would be delighted for our daughter to achieve so magnificent a match. At the same time, as her parents and responsible for her well-being all her life so far, we feel we must point out that our daughter is a tender young person of little or no experience with the rough ways of the world, whereas you yourself, Sir – Sire – are a powerful and dominant physical presence. We fear that overcome with passion and in the heat of your affection you might unintentionally do her some injury. Is it possible, do you think, that you might have your claws removed and your teeth extracted? We would be much happier, and would surely have no qualms about receiving your proposal again if you did.' The lion, willing to do anything at all to be able to wed the damsel, at once made off to the nearest surgeon-dentist. Clawless and toothless he soon returned once more to the girl's parents, where he presented himself again as a humble suitor. The parents laughed in his face and showed him the door, telling him to do his worst. A sadder and wiser lion departed, thinking that 'Even the strongest of the strong can become the weakest of the weak through love.'

THE PROPHETIC CAT

'A cat washing on the doorstep means a visit.'
Sri Lankan proverb

CATCALL

THE CATCALL today in English is a jeer of derision, a whistle through the teeth intended to convey dissatisfaction, a means of barracking a performance. And it is in that latter sense that the expression originated. For in the 1650s a catcall was a hand-held device that, when blown into, produced an unpleasantly high-pitched sound that was held to mimic the voice of a mocking cat. It was used in playhouses, when blown by an actor off-stage, to indicate when it was appropriate for the audience to voice their disapproval, much as pantomime audiences today are encouraged to boo and hiss the villain.

Seventeenth-century English audiences loved this invitation to participate. In fact, they went completely overboard for it, and within a few years were bringing their own catcall devices to playhouses. Samuel Pepys, the diarist, for example, bought himself a catcall with which to amuse himself and his friends: it cost him two groats (eight pence or one thirtieth of a pound).

Forty years later in London, it was impossible to get through a theatrical performance without the audience at one stage or another (or more often) interrupting the proceedings by using their catcalls. It is likely that the practice also gave rise to the noun 'caterwauling'.

THE BOBCAT

'BOBCAT' is the ordinary (non-technical) word in the USA for the North American lynx or wildcat, *Felis rufus* or *Lynx rufus*, also known as the bay lynx or red lynx. (It is not, however, the same as the slightly larger Canada lynx.) There are 12 recognized subspecies of bobcat which, between them, range from southern Canada to northern Mexico. Their most distinctive characteristics are black bars on the forelegs and a black-tipped stubby tail. It is the tail that may well have evoked the name 'bobcat' – the word 'bob' was first recorded in English in 1615 to mean 'short, stubby, and rather rounded' – although the overall body shape (relatively small in relation to legs and paws) might have been equally influential. Most active in the hours of twilight and dawn, the bobcat's preferred diet is of rabbits and hares, although it will hunt and eat anything from small deer to rodents and insects.

HOLD THAT TIGER!

'To bathe a cat takes brute force, perseverance, courage of conviction – and a cat. The last ingredient is usually hardest to come by.'
STEPHEN BAKER, author of *How to Live with a Neurotic Cat*

SEA CATS

The marine otter or sea cat (*Lontra felina*) – known in Spanish apparently as the *chungungo* or *chinchimen* – is not the same as the sea otter (*Enhydra lutris*). Only 90 centimetres (three feet) long, it is the smallest marine mammal in the world. It is known as the sea cat because of its sleek forehead, wide, fur-covered nose and large whiskers. Its range is along the Pacific coast from northern Peru right down to the southern tip of South America, and in isolated pockets up the Atlantic  coast of Argentina. It likes rocky shores and tidal cliff caves, for although it is much more agile in the water, it is also an excellent rock climber on land. Currently, sea cats are a highly endangered species.

APPLAUSE FOR CLAWS

A CAT'S CLAWS are not just for protection. They are what the cat walks on, assist in grooming and stretching, and fine-tune the ability to balance on precarious surfaces. The surgical declawing of a cat – still a practice in some countries – thus robs a cat of some of its most valuable faculties. In fact, the loss may be not just physical but psychological, and lead to the equivalent of clinical depression in a human.

OSCAR, ANGEL OF DEATH

Oscar is a cat in a nursing home in Providence, Rhode Island, who apparently has the ability to tell when a patient in the home's advanced dementia unit is about to pass away. When the time comes, he tends to go to the patient's room, jump up onto the bed, curl up alongside the patient, and purr. So often has he done this, and so regularly has the patient peacefully died anything from one to six hours later, that the staff of the nursing home have come to treat his action as an early warning, and have been able to advise the patient's family that they should attend as soon as possible. And yet Oscar is only a young cat – although he is undoubtedly streetwise, for he was brought in to the nursing home from an animal shelter.

So how does Oscar know? It may be that the cat is sensing the 'smell' of death so beloved of crime-writers – it is, after all, possible that certain chemical substances are released in the body shortly before death, and the cat is scenting them. Or Oscar may be finely attuned to the slowing respiration of dying patients. Alternatively, the cat may have noted how the nursing home staff tend to pay special attention to a patient they know is dying. Oscar may have begun mimicking the custom, only even more sensitively.

PAWS & PAWNS

There is an old European folk tale that tells how very much monkeys love roast chestnuts. But the trouble with chestnuts roasting in a pan over an open fire is that they are hot – too hot to touch – yet only delicious to eat when they *are* hot. So, the folk tale goes, the monkeys sought someone gullible or desperate enough to agree to take the chestnuts off the fire and pass them over to the monkeys. They finally lighted upon a cat, who agreed to take on the task. The cat burned its paws dreadfully, but having agreed to do it, did it (and no doubt hurried off to the vet to invest its hard-earned payment in treatment for its paws).

The tale represents the origin of the English word *catspaw* – meaning someone who is 'used' by a more dominant personality to get something done that the dominant personality does not wish to do. Even more interestingly, it points up the linguistic relationship between *paws* and *pawns* – the most menial pieces in play in a game of chess. For pawns were intended on the chessboard to correspond to *foot*-soldiers (modern French *pions* or 'pawns', from Latin *pediones*) who in peacetime might have to turn their hand to anything to stay alive, even becoming manual labourers – which is why chess pawns tend to be 'farmworkers' in Germanic languages.

In Lewis Carroll's (*Alice*) *Through the Looking-Glass*, the young Alice is supposed to be a white pawn in a game of chess. And of course, one of the rules of chess is that if a pawn reaches the final rank, it becomes a queen – the most powerful piece, certainly threatening a king.

Which leads on to another English expression: 'A cat may look at a king'. This is an expression that linguistic historians have puzzled over for centuries, particularly when used as a political statement by potential rebels in England in 1652, although apparently derived from a proverb of a century earlier. Some say that a story of Aesop contains the germ of the notion; others claim that it was a proverb in Dutch or a Mother Goose nursery rhyme first.

But the French equivalent is rather different, and revealing: *un chien regarde bien un évêque* 'a dog may well look at a bishop'. Bishops, kings – we are surely still talking about the game of chess here. And dogs have paws as much as cats – indeed, in English it would not be impossible for a dog to be described as a 'catspaw' if used as an accomplice by a human criminal – so we are also talking both of paws and pawns. Pawns that may not only look at a bishop or a king but rule the land as a dominant queen.

At the end of *Through the Looking-Glass*, Alice is hailed as a second white queen, and eventually captures – or at least takes hold of – the red queen.

The major show breeds of cats are:

Abyssinian.	Javanese . . . .
American Curl Longhair	Korat . . . .
American Curl Shorthair	Maine Coon . . . .
American Shorthair	Manx . . . .
American Wirehair	Non-pedigree . . . .
Angora	Norwegian Forest Cat/ . . . .
Balinese	Siberian Forest Cat . . . .
Bengal	Ocicat. . . . .
Birman	Oriental Shorthair . . . .
Bombay	Persian Longhair . . . .
British Shorthair.	Ragdoll. . . . .
Burmese	Scottish Fold Longhair/Shorthair . .
Burmilla	Selkirk Rex. . . . .
California Spangled	Siamese. . . . .
Chartreux.	Singapura . . . .
Cornish Rex/Devon Rex	Snowshoe. . . . .
Cymric.	Somali . . . .
European Shorthair	Sphynx . . . .
Egyptian Mau	Tiffanie . . . .
Exotic.	Tonkinese. . . . .
Havana	Turkish Angora. . . . .
Japanese Bobtail	Turkish Van . . . .

WHY THE MANX CAT HAS NO TAIL

On the Isle of Man – which is the home of the Manx cat – they say that the Manx cat lost its tail entirely through its own silly fault. It was the time of the Flood, and Noah had set up a strict schedule for animals to enter the Ark two by two. But one or both of the Manx cats – at that time with tails like all other cats – dallied outside, looking at the torrents of water streaming down, for it was, of course, raining cats and, er, other animals. Eventually, when the Manx cats were the only creatures not to have boarded the Ark and the embarkation deadline was in danger, Noah lost his patience and slammed the Ark door shut. But the one or both Manx cats were even quicker. Like, er, cats, they sprang inside at the last moment – but the door slammed on their tails. Legend has it that Manx cats have had no tails ever since.

THE CAT O' NINE TAILS was a cruel sort of whip used to discipline disobedient rank-and-file sailors from the late seventeenth century to the early nineteenth. It was a fearsome object, consisting of a thickish rope handle from which sprang nine viciously knotted cords or strands. It was the knots in the whip strands that caused the most pain and the most harm to the backs of sailors to which it was forcefully applied. For the knots left long, deep scratches, as if the sailors had been attacked by a large and heavily clawed cat. Hence the name (in German, *neunschwänzige Katze*; in Italian, *gatto a nove code*).

During the 1990s there was a lengthy burst of correspondence to the London *Times* on the subject of why the whip should have had nine tails. The main question was over whether it had anything to do with the notion that cats had nine lives. (Since cats *don't* have nine lives in Italy, this suggestion, at least in that country, was a non-starter.)

In fact, there is a very obvious and practical reason. Nautical ropes (and ropes for other purposes, such as bell-ringing) are mostly made up of three strands or cords spliced (plaited) together. Individual ropes are not particularly thick, but if you wanted to fashion a thick handle, you might well splice together three whole ropes (that is, all together, nine strands). Having fashioned your handle to a required length, you would then have three three-stranded ropes protruding from your handle, which you then would unpick and separate into nine strands, knotting them appropriately, to make the whip.

IN 1840s BRITAIN, a 'cat' was criminal slang for a lady's muff – a fur cylinder into which a lady might pop her hands to keep them warm during a journey. A muff might well look like a cat sitting on the lady's lap, but might well additionally contain other things, such as small items of jewellery. By the 1930s in the USA, the definition had extended to include any fashion accessory covered in fur, at a time when furry items were expensive luxuries and were similar targets for pickpockets and muggers.

✻ A female cat reaches sexual maturity between the ages of only six and ten months. A male cat normally reaches sexual maturity between the ages of nine and 12 months.

✻ Female cats are polyoestrous – that is, a cat may experience many periods of preparedness for sexual congress ('heat', or oestrous) over a single year. Each period of oestrous lasts a minimum of four days. If the cat is not impregnated by the end of that time, the period of oestrous may continue for up to six more days. If the cat is impregnated, however, no more periods of oestrous occur until after the birth.

✻ During a period of oestrus, a female cat may participate in sex with a number of different male cats, some of whom may fight each other for the privilege. Alternatively, some female cats prefer to restrict their mating to just one or two male partners.

✻ The act of sex itself lasts between one and four minutes. It takes between five and 15 minutes for a male, after mating once, to be able to mate again, the length of time increasing after each consecutive engagement.

✻ Female cats have evolved to be 'super-fecund', which means that each kitten of a litter of kittens may have a different father. This is because the repeated act of sex actually releases further eggs from the ovaries that may be fertilized.

✻ Even if a female cat is pregnant, she may continue to have sex with male cats until as late as three-quarters of the way through pregnancy.

✻ Pregnancy for a female cat lasts approximately nine weeks, or between 62 and 65 days from conception to giving birth.

————— FIX & RELEASE —————

This system was pioneered in the 1980s by various charitable organizations in Britain (including the Royal Society for the Prevention of Cruelty to Animals). It has since been taken up by similar organizations elsewhere in the world, notably in North America (where the system may alternatively be known as fix and return). It involves trapping feral cats on large business estates or other semi-rural areas, giving them a full veterinary examination, spaying or neutering them, vaccinating them against many common diseases (especially cat flu), allowing them some comfortable convalescence time, and returning them to the locations they came from. Some organizations also microchip the cats for later identification if necessary.

The system has greatly reduced the numbers of stray feral cats that were once simply put down, and has also relieved what had become intolerable pressure on cat shelters to house limitless quantities of adult cats left on their doorstep.

THE PANTHER

Technically, 'panther' is not the name of any specific animal. In fact, it is either the name of the genus that includes lions, tigers, leopards and jaguars, or, in the expression 'black panther', it refers to melanistic leopards or jaguars. Nonetheless, in many parts of the world, 'panther' can be used as a general term for large wildcats such as pumas and cougars (mountain lions) even if, as in some rural areas of the USA, it is more commonly used in the dialectal form of 'painter'.

All the same, the chances are that the original meaning of the word – before the ancient Greek and Sanskrit terms related to it, before even the ancient Egyptian term apparently akin to it – was 'tiger'.

GROOM FOR IMPROVEMENT

Cats, especially female cats, are said to spend something like 30% of their waking life grooming themselves, which involves licking their fur. Amazingly, they lose almost as much body liquid in the form of saliva when they are grooming themselves as they do through normal urination.

NIN, THE OBSERVATORY CAT

FOR MORE THAN ELEVEN YEARS until the end of 2007, Nin – a mostly white ex-stray cat – was a resident mouse-catcher and mascot of the generally fog-shrouded non-profit meteorological observatory on Mount Washington, 6,288 feet (1,916.6 metres) up on the highest peak in the White Mountains of New Hampshire, USA, proudly advertised as 'home of the world's worst weather'. During that time, Nin had most willingly subjected himself to pampering and petting by tourists and researchers alike, becoming a celebrity and – by being depicted on a Mount Washington Observatory Shop souvenir mug, price US$10 – a fund-raiser.

No one will say whether Nin was named after the Catalan-Cuban-French diarist and writer of female erotica Anaïs Nin (1903–77), but it has always been vehemently denied – no matter how appropriate the suggestion might have seemed – that the name was instead an abbreviation of 'nincompoop'.

CAT & KITTENS FULL OF ALE

IN 1820s BRITAIN and in 1860s USA, a 'cat and kittens' was a slang term for a set of pewter ale-mugs comprising a number of pint-pots, holding one pint (UK 0.568 litre; US 0.473 liter) and one quart-pot (two pints, a quarter of a gallon: UK 1.136 litre; US 0.946 liter).

KIT-CAT SIZE

28 in

36 in

'KIT-CAT SIZE' is a description from the international world of fine art and refers to a type of painted portrait, specifically one that features a subject's head and chest and at least one of the hands, but which is a good deal smaller than in real life. The description is derived from the portraits of the members of the Kit-Cat Club – Whig politicians, men of letters, artists and actors who first convened in the pie-house owned and run by one Christopher Catling ('Kit Cat', creator of the Kit-Kat mutton pie) in the early 1700s in Shire Lane by Temple Bar, in London – and especially the 48 portraits by royal court painter Sir Godfrey Kneller in what became a standard frame format of 36 by 28 inches (91.44 by 71.12 centimetres). This size was apparently necessitated by the restricted wall space available for hanging the portraits under the original pie-house's low ceiling.

LION-SPOTTING

THE MODERN LION, *Panthera leo*, 'in the wild' is now mainly restricted to national safari parks and wildlife reserves in southern, central and eastern Africa, although some roam in less restrictive but more stressful conditions in western India. Until recent times there were several subspecies of lion, notably in what is now Saudi Arabia and Iran, although now all these are extinct – except for a small number of individual Barbary lions (*Panthera leo leo*), alternatively called Atlas or Nubian lions, which have, over the past thirty years, been discovered in zoos and circuses around the world, and which have since been subject to attempts to collect them all together and conserve them.

AESOP'S FABLE OF THE LION & THE BOAR

It was a hot summer day in a dry and dusty region of Africa. The animals at one remote water-hole scattered regretfully when they saw a lion and a boar approaching from different directions. Both thus reached the deserted water's edge at the same moment. Neither would let the other drink before him, and a bloody battle for supremacy ensued. It went on and on, though both lion and boar quickly became tired and sore from their wounds. Finally, by unspoken agreement, they sat back and panted for a while. And as they did, they spotted the vultures circling patiently overhead, waiting to dine on the eventual loser. The battle was at once forgotten, for both lion and boar saw it was infinitely preferable to stay alive and drink together than to become food for vultures.

A newborn kitten's eyes may open as quickly as in two days, although more often it does not happen until around the eighth or ninth day. And it takes two weeks for kittens to be able to hear properly – although they become aware of the vibrations of their mother's purring well before that.

—————————— THE NON-SCRIPTURAL CAT ——————————

The cat is the only domestic animal not mentioned in the Bible.

—————————— POLECAT SONGS ——————————

All right – a polecat is not a cat but (properly speaking) a member of the European badger/weasel family, the Mustelidae. All the same, the Polecat songs have nothing to do with polecats either. They are the twelve part-songs every serious barbershop singer knows at least one part to, and are so called because, in theory, they are best known for being sung under the cat's head carved at the top of the barber's pole.

—————————— CAT-WHIPPER'S ALLEY ——————————

In the Ostrobothnian coastal town mostly called by its Swedish name, Kristinestad, because it is in the mainly Swedish-speaking part of Finland, there is a neatly preserved grid of old wooden houses on a hillside above a riverbank. Towards one side of this lies a narrow street that, partly because of its name, is renowned specifically as the third-narrowest still-used thoroughfare in Finland and much photographed by tourists and travel agents. It is called *Kattpiskargränden* – or in Finnish, *Kissanpiiskaajankuja* – 'the cat-whipper's alley', although it is often more mischievously translated as 'cat-spanker's alley'. Some say that there was once a plague of feral cats in this area, and the community had to employ a cat-elimination officer. The alternative and rather more accepted theory is perhaps unlikelier still. It seems that much of the old town was originally built by unpleasantly truculent labourers from a neighbouring settlement called Skaftung, and that these Skaftungers – 'Kattungilaisia', to the Finns (who have never liked pronouncing adjoining consonants) – when they went on the rampage, as they often did, had to be regularly disciplined. And thanks to the Finnish term for them, they became known as 'cats' in Swedish – which was then retranslated back into Finnish for the name of the alley.